ACADEMIC LIBRARIES AND TOXIC LEADERSHIP

CHANDOS
INFORMATION PROFESSIONAL SERIES
Series Editor: Ruth Rikowski
(email: Rikowskigr@aol.com)

Chandos' new series of books is aimed at the busy information professional. They have been specially commissioned to provide the reader with an authoritative view of current thinking. They are designed to provide easy-to-read and (most importantly) practical coverage of topics that are of interest to librarians and other information professionals. If you would like a full listing of current and forthcoming titles, please visit www.chandospublishing.com.

New authors: we are always pleased to receive ideas for new titles; if you would like to write a book for Chandos, please contact Dr Glyn Jones on g.jones.2@elsevier.com or telephone +44 (0) 1865 843000.

ACADEMIC LIBRARIES AND TOXIC LEADERSHIP

ALMA C. ORTEGA

CHANDOS PUBLISHING

An imprint of Elsevier • elsevier.com

Chandos Publishing is an imprint of Elsevier
50 Hampshire Street, 5th Floor, Cambridge, MA 02139, United States
The Boulevard, Langford Lane, Kidlington, OX5 1GB, United Kingdom

Notices

Knowledge and best practice in this field are constantly changing. As new research and
experience broaden our understanding, changes in research methods, professional practices, or
medical treatment may become necessary.

Practitioners and researchers must always rely on their own experience and knowledge in
evaluating and using any information, methods, compounds, or experiments described herein.
In using such information or methods they should be mindful of their own safety and the safety
of others, including parties for whom they have a professional responsibility.

To the fullest extent of the law, neither the Publisher nor the authors, contributors, or editors,
assume any liability for any injury and/or damage to persons or property as a matter of products
liability, negligence or otherwise, or from any use or operation of any methods, products,
instructions, or ideas contained in the material herein.

British Library Cataloguing-in-Publication Data
A catalogue record for this book is available from the British Library

Library of Congress Cataloging-in-Publication Data
A catalog record for this book is available from the Library of Congress

ISBN: 978-0-08-100637-5 (print)
ISBN: 978-0-08-100650-4 (online)

For information on all Chandos Publishing publications visit
our website at https://www.elsevier.com/books-and-journals

Working together
to grow libraries in
developing countries

www.elsevier.com • www.bookaid.org

Publisher: Glyn Jones
Acquisition Editor: Glyn Jones
Editorial Project Manager: Lindsay Lawrence
Production Project Manager: Priya Kumaraguruparan
Designer: Victoria Pearson

Typeset by MPS Limited, Chennai, India

CONTENTS

PREFACE

This book was inspired by what has happened to many academic librarians. Academic libraries as part of a university or college are seen as a piece of the puzzle of higher education, but they are really never thought about (unless it is accreditation time). They are not in the consciousness of most administrators, or even of most students. They know the academic library as a service, they call anyone inside the library building a librarian. Many of them do not know a master's degree is needed to become a librarian; much less do they know that many of these librarians are faculty members at their institutions. Therefore, it is not surprising to learn that they have no idea of (or interest in) how an academic library is managed, much less led

Academic libraries are dynamic and made up of multiple departments or units, all dependent on each other to best serve the university community. But when a toxic leader is in charge of any aspect of the library's units, it is then that issues arise. This is more than a simple personality clash; this is about an actual, toxic, library leader, someone in it for themselves, regardless of the harm they cause the library, its librarians, its staff, and its services to students, faculty, and the university community at large.

I have been thanked and congratulated on my bravery. I do not consider myself brave, I consider myself an academic librarian who merely wants to humanize the profession so that others may finally understand that academic librarians are more than the services they provide, that we are people who care about research and the research process, and who also care about having a good quality of life in the workplace.

Academic libraries are an essential resource in higher education. We cannot let a few bad leaders—though some would say it is well more than a few—to continue corrupting leadership in academic libraries. It is time to address this urgent leadership issue if we want to be equipped for the challenges still awaiting academic libraries, challenges beyond the relentless need to prove the value of the academic library and being asked to continue doing more with less funding year after year. The decline in effective leadership in libraries in general, and more so in academic libraries, is a serious matter that deserves and needs to be thoroughly discussed. If we cannot be critical of ourselves to improve an obvious leadership gap in our own profession, then who will?

I hope you find this book helpful in learning about toxic leadership, and about academic libraries and toxic leadership.

INTRODUCTION: WHY THE RESEARCH ON ACADEMIC LIBRARIES AND TOXIC LEADERSHIP?

Academic libraries are usually described as places for research and study, and rarely does academic literature, or even informal literature (such as professional blogs) acknowledge the possibility of dysfunction and toxicity in relationships between upper management of libraries, on the one hand, and librarians or other library support staff, on the other. The topic of toxic leadership in academic libraries has been an interest of mine since late 2005. Over the years, I have spent time speaking to academic librarian colleagues about adverse leadership in their libraries. I have spoken primarily with women, because over 82% of professional librarians are women (DPE Research Department, 2011).

Most of these academic librarians mentioned the occasional bully at a library, yet not necessarily in their own library. Some librarians did share information about more serious situations and used terms such as *psychopaths*, *mean-games*, and *dysfunctional*, among others, to describe the situations in which they worked or the people they were forced to work with. When asked what the library management (including Human Resources) was doing to address these issues, most were not aware of anything being done to ameliorate or end the abuse. In their experience, toxic leadership leading to a toxic environment was something almost everyone in academic libraries knows about, but it is not openly discussed. This anecdotal information is troubling and identified a phenomenon that can be observed in certain academic libraries.

It would be a few more years before a blog post addressing toxic leadership in libraries, by Abram (2011), candidly mentioned bullying in libraries:

> This year, while working with librarians who are in the early stages of their career I was appalled to hear about some terrible (and often unaddressed) incidents of professional and workplace bullying by co-workers, management and users. Just scratch a group of library workers and the stories pour out.

With this blog post, anecdotal information, which up to then had been shared quietly among librarians, was now openly reported on social media. Abram (2011) concluded his blog entry with the following statement: "People should have grown up enough as adults that it shouldn't happen — or at least bullying should be addressed properly in our field and workplaces." It was this last phrase that confirmed that the research I desire to do was, indeed, warranted. There had been previous professional articles which at least hinted at toxic environments and toxic leadership in public libraries and special libraries (Proctor, 2001; Schachter, 2008), but there is a dearth of information about toxic leadership in academic libraries. Owing to their centrality to academic institutions and their unique context there is a need to comprehensively explore the topic of toxic leadership in academic libraries.

Aggression and bullying at work can be symptoms of a broader problem, the inability of library administrators to address behavior that is detrimental to the organization. Unscrupulous behaviors toward employees can create a toxic environment in any workplace. Several authors have addressed the connection between organizational leadership and cultures that foster bullying (Kellerman, 2004; Lipman-Blumen, 2005a; Reed, 2004; Whicker, 1996). The lack of research regarding dysfunctional and toxic environments in academic libraries and the scarcity of publications about how to be a good leader in libraries reveal that to better understand toxic behaviors, the structural causes that enable such behaviors need to be explored.

Toxic leadership is in every organization, including academic libraries, whether we would like to acknowledge it or not. Toxic leadership is a phenomenon that exists in contemporary organizations, resulting in an ineffective and less productive work environment (Frost, 2003; Kusy & Holloway, 2009; Lipman-Blumen, 2005a; Sutton, 2010). The prevalent lack of positive leadership that leads to poor workplace climates and cultures has led some researchers to assert that toxic leadership is a fact of organizational life (Frost, 2003; Kusy & Holloway, 2009).

Toxic leadership is frequently part and parcel of a constellation of more general characteristics of the contemporary workplace. Porath and Pearson (2013) concluded that "rudeness at work is rampant, and it's on the rise" (p. 116). They documented that incivility issues have an effect on work output and quality of life in the United States and Canada; they recently noted, "Over the past 14 years we have polled thousands of workers about how they're treated on the job, and 98% have reported experiencing uncivil behavior" (p. 116). These types of occurrences are not limited to corporate America; academic environments are not immune to insidious workplace behavior, workplace aggression, abusive supervision, relational aggression, incivility, intimidation and bullying, all of which are associated with toxic leadership (Dellasega, 2011; Lipman-Blumen, 2005a; Pelletier, 2010, 2012; Porath & Pearson, 2013; Reed, 2014; Schmidt, 2007, 2014; Spector & Rodopman, 2010; Sutton, 2010; Tepper, 2000).

Behaviors, such as aggression and bullying, which lead to a toxic workplace environment within the academy have only recently been discussed and documented in the academic literature, even though some scholars suggest these offenses have been on the rise for the past decade (Coyne, 2011; Fratzl & McKay, 2013; Keashly & Neuman, 2010; Klein & Lester, 2013; Twale & De Luca, 2008). A toxic environment leads to the loss of talented faculty members and a decline in productivity in those who remain and are affected emotionally, psychologically and/or physically (Brouwer, Koopmanschap, & Rutten, 1997; Klein & Lester, 2013; Organ, 1997; Tracy, Lutgen-Sandvik, & Alberts, 2006). Academic libraries are a specific type of higher education setting, yet their work environments have received little attention and the role that leadership plays in creating and sustaining productive and unproductive conditions has been virtually ignored.

Part of the research data used to write this book came from a national online survey that was administered over a period of 6 weeks on professional academic librarians' lists in the United States and abroad, as well as follow-up survey interviews and in-depth interviews for this book. This book documents academic librarians who had to work with a toxic leader or witnessed toxic leadership, and it also expands on the findings of the national study and aspires to open the conversation on toxic leadership, and leadership in general, in academic libraries.

ORGANIZATION OF THIS BOOK

Chapter 1: *What is Leadership? What is Toxic Leadership?* introduces the topic of leadership and mentions that in what little research has been done on library and information studies, leadership has been seen only as a positive event. Only recently have scholars in the field addressed the need to study the impact of negative leadership in academic libraries (Hernon & Pors, 2013). This has shown up in the guise of bad, incompetent, leadership with negative actions, but the term "toxic leadership" has yet to be used in the library and information studies field. The second half of the chapter presents a definition of "toxic leadership" from the author, based on the reported experiences of academic librarians as well as how it has been identified in the literature of leadership studies and library and information studies. Chapter 2: *How to Acknowledge the Presence of Toxic Leadership* discusses the effects of toxic leadership in organizations in general and then presents its effects on academic libraries and librarians as well as User Services.

In Chapter 3: *What to Do about Toxic Leadership?* information about the situation after toxic leadership has been recognized, and how to begin to counteract toxic leadership, is provided, including what steps to take when confronted with toxic leadership in the workplace. Who to talk to, and the consequences of inaction, are also discussed. Chapter 4: *Regaining Control of the Library* is about the difficult task—taking over your library. It must be done in order to improve morale and help those who are suffering the most. The chapter also discusses the important topic of maintaining a toxic leader-free library; because after the toxic leader/s (or immediate threat) has been removed (or isolated), the situation will not change for the better on its own. Unless mechanisms have been put in place to prevent the rise of another toxic leader, the situation that has just been resolved could arise again in the near future.

Chapter 5: *The Healing Process for the Academic Library free of Toxic Leaders* deals with the healing process, which varies from academic library to academic library, and is usually influenced by its parent institution. Many librarians reported seeking professional assistance from psychologists or career counselors to focus their energies in a positive direction, while still others began taking up old or new hobbies, to wean themselves from the destructive mechanisms they adopted to cope while they were working under a tyrant. The chapter also discusses residual toxicity, which can become an ongoing problem for some librarians if the healing process is not undertaken. Chapter 6: *Cases* illustrates how toxic leadership was experienced and handled at a variety of colleges and universities across the United States. Toxic leadership is present at all types of academic libraries and levels of administration, whether it be community colleges or prestigious, large, research-intensive universities.

REFERENCES

Abram, S. (2011). Bullying: Personal, professional and Workplace [Blog post]. Retrieved from <http://stephenslighthouse.com/2011/07/07/bullying-personal-professional-and-workplace/>.

Brouwer, W. F. B., Koopmanschap, M. A., & Rutten, F. F. H. (1997). Productivity costs in cost-effectiveness analysis: Numerator or denominator: A further discussion. *Health Informatics*, *6*, 511–514.

Coyne, I. (2011). Bullying in the workplace. In C. P. Monks, & I. Coyne (Eds.), *Bullying in different contexts* (pp. 157–184). New York, NY: Cambridge University Press.

Dellasega, C. (2011). *When nurses hurt nurses. Recognizing and overcoming the cycle of bullying.* Indianapolis, IN: Sigma Theta Tau International.

DPE Research Department. (2011). Library workers: Facts and figures. Retrieved from <http://ala-apa.org/files/2012/03/Library-Workers-2011.pdf>.

Fratzl, J., & McKay, R. (2013). Professional staff in academia: Academic culture and the role of aggression. In J. Lester (Ed.), *Workplace bullying in higher education* (pp. 60–73). New York, NY: Routledge.

Frost, P. J. (2003). *Toxic emotions at work: How compassionate managers handle pain and conflict.* Boston, MA: Harvard Business School Press.

Hernon, P., & Pors, N. O. (2013). Leadership as viewed across countries. In P. Hernon, & N. O. Pors (Eds.), *Library leadership in the United States and Europe: Comparative study of academic and public libraries* (pp. 191–204). Santa Barbara, CA: Libraries Unlimited.

Keashly, L., & Neuman, J. H. (2010). Faculty experiences with bullying in higher education: Causes, consequences, and management. *Administrative Theory & Praxis*, *32*(1), 48–70.

Kellerman, B. (2004). *Bad leadership: What it is, how it happens, why it matters.* Boston, MA: Harvard Business School Press.

Klein, C., & Lester, J. (2013). Moving beyond awareness and tolerance: Recommendations and implications for workplace bullying in higher education. In J. Lester (Ed.), *Workplace bullying in higher education* (pp. 138–147). New York, NY: Routledge.

Kusy, M. E., & Holloway, E. L. (2009). *Toxic workplace!: Managing toxic personalities and their systems of power.* San Francisco: Jossey-Bass.

Lipman-Blumen, J. (2005a). The allure of toxic leaders: Why followers rarely escape their clutches. *Ivey Business Journal*, *69*(3), 1–8.

Organ, D. W. (1997). Organizational citizenship behavior: It's construct clean-up time. *Human Performance*, *10*(2), 85–97.

Pelletier, K. L. (2010). Leader toxicity: An empirical investigation of toxic behavior and rhetoric. *Leadership*, *6*(4), 373–389.

Pelletier, K. L. (2012). Perceptions of and reactions to leader toxicity: Do leader-follower relationships and identification with victim matter?. *Leadership Quarterly*, *23*, 412–424.

Porath, C., & Pearson, C. M. (2013). The price of incivility: Lack of respect hurts morale—and the bottom line. *Harvard Business Review*, *91*(1/2), 114–121.

Proctor, R. (2001). A personnel time bomb. *Public Library Journal*, *16*(3), 69–70.

Reed, G. E. (2004). Toxic leadership. *Military Review*, *84*(4), 67–71.

Reed, G. E. (2014). Toxic leadership, unit climate, and organizational effectiveness. *Air & Space Power Journal*. Retrieved from http://www.airpower.au.af.mil/apjinternational/apj-s/2014/2014-3/2014_3_03_reed_s_eng.pdf.

Schachter, D. (2008). Learn to embrace opposition for improved decision making. *Information Outlook*, *12*(10), 44–45.

Schmidt, A. A. (2008). *Development and validation of toxic leadership scale.* Master's Thesis University of Maryland at College Park.

Schmidt, A. A. (2014). An examination of toxic leadership, job outcomes, and the impact of military deployment *(Unpublished doctoral dissertation).* University of Maryland, College Park.

Spector, P. E., & Rodopman, O. B. (2010). Methodological issues in studying insidious workplace behavior. In J. Greenberg (Ed.), *Insidious workplace behavior* (pp. 273–306). New York, NY: Routledge.

Sutton, R. I. (2010). *The no asshole rule: Building a civilized workplace and surviving one that isn't.* New York, NY: Business Plus.

Tepper, B. J. (2000). Consequences of abusive supervision. *Academy of Management Journal, 43*(2), 178–190.

Tracy, S. J., Lutgen-Sandvik, P., & Alberts, J. K. (2006). Nightmares, demons and slaves: Exploring the painful metaphors of workplace bullying. *Management Communication Quarterly, 20*(2), 1–38.

Twale, D. J., & De Luca, B. M. (2008). *Faculty incivility: The rise of the academic bully culture and what to do about it.* San Francisco, CA: Jossey-Bass.

Whicker, M. L. (1996). *Toxic leaders: When organizations go bad.* Westport, CT: Quorum Books.

CHAPTER 1

What Is Leadership?
What Is Toxic Leadership?

1.1 DEFINING LEADERSHIP

The field of Leadership Studies has had a long time now to define itself, yet those engaged in it seem to have been unable to do so. There are many ways of looking at leadership, from the viewpoint of the Great Man Theory, now seen as antiquated, to that of the closely related "leadership traits" theory, to those of the transactional leadership and the transformational leadership styles. Then there are the ethical, servant, authentic, intentional, and collaborative leadership philosophies and management practices, and last but not least, practical methods to make effective leaders, and on top of that of course, the new models of leadership that have yet to emerge.

According to Riggs (2001), "Throughout the world, leadership is generally perceived as something we need more of, while at the same time it is generally misunderstood. There are at least 100 definitions of leadership." (p. 5). Mavranic (2005) declared that "Leadership is a relationship between leaders and followers, both individual and group, in mutual pursuit of organizational outcomes and in the fulfillment of individual wants and needs" (p. 394). As has been seen, leadership can be explained simply, without convoluting the concept. There are countless definitions of leadership, but in the end, leadership is whatever the leader of an organization makes it, as long as it has a positive result. If the leader has a strong work ethic and cares about their organization, then there will be effective changes, whereas if the leader is not ethical or caring but is narcissistic or amoral, then the consequences for the organization will not be positive because "The quality of the leadership, more than any other single factor, determines the success or failure of an organization" (Fiedler & Chemers, 1984). This is why it is important that leadership be understood even in just a simple manner at first, because this is a basis for the understanding of leadership to expand and become more complex. The more one reads about leadership, the more one realizes there is to the topic.

Academic Libraries and Toxic Leadership.
DOI: http://dx.doi.org/10.1016/B978-0-08-100637-5.00001-7

Burns (1978), in his seminal book *Leadership*, presented the now well-known transactional leadership and transformational leadership styles. He also bemoaned the fact that leadership studies had branched into areas focusing respectively on leaders and followers, while it is the interaction between the two that allows leadership to occur. In this he recognized the importance of followership in leadership. Without followers there are no leaders of any type, positive or negative. By this definition leadership is an ongoing process which, if carried out well, with good intentions, creates positive change for the organization and everyone working there. A leader needs followers and followers need a leader who is visionary and has a plan for the organization and its employees. Leaders do not only develop subordinates, they also create better outcomes for the organization as a whole, including themselves.

Leadership, in the context of this book, may have a different meaning for some readers. It is straightforward to conceive of a leader who cares for and protects subordinates, while still carrying out the mission of the academic library; an in-tune leader, who sees trouble before it starts, who works on preventive measures, and ways of immediately tackling a problem or approaching troubled employees, sometimes even a co-worker. A leader who is present and faces challenges without affecting the workflow or *esprit de corps* of the workplace is exceptional. These leaders indeed exist, but, unfortunately, are not as plentiful as many academic librarians would hope, going by the research undertaken to write this book. There are still many engaged library leaders who work with committed academic librarians, which makes for a successful leadership experience in academic libraries for everyone involved, from the leader to the librarians to the users. This is why leadership is an important topic that needs to be discussed completely, from every angle, in academic libraries.

It is easy to define leadership simply as taking responsibility for one's actions and those of one's subordinates. Leadership comes down to taking charge and acting responsibly in many types of circumstances. The leader is not a coward, but she or he knows when to take risks and accept challenges, as well as when to hold back, so as to avoid a negative impact on the organization. These challenges can range from maintaining or improving library services or a library department to dealing with a leadership crisis. Without a leader who knows how to identify a crisis, then poor leadership is almost surely to occur, owing to unintentional mishaps. Good leaders know how to differentiate a crisis from a minor incident. A crisis may necessitate diplomacy and quickly formed plans of action, not just following through a set procedure, which is typically how minor incidents are resolved.

Leadership is usually associated with positive outcomes for a country, an organization, and individuals. To assist you in learning more about what leadership is, how it is defined, depending on the organizational need, and how to apply it to your organization or yourself, a brief reading list is presented here:

1. *Leadership* by James McGregor Burns
2. *On Leadership* by John William Gardner
3. *On Becoming a Leader* by Warren G. Bennis
4. *Deep Change: Discovering the Leader Within* by Robert E. Quinn
5. *The Leadership Challenge: How to Make Extraordinary Things Happen in Organizations* by James M. Kouzes and Barry Z. Posner
6. *Leadership and the New Science: Discovering Order in a Chaotic World* by Margaret J. Wheatley
7. *Servant Leadership: A Journey into the Nature of Legitimate Power and Greatness* by Robert K. Greenleaf
8. *Leadership Classics* edited by J. Timothy McMahon
9. *Good to Great: Why Some Companies Make the Leap...and Others Don't* by Jim Collins
10. *The Fifth Discipline: The Art and Practice of the Learning Organization* by Peter M. Senge

This is obviously not an exhaustive list, but it allows you explore the many aspects of leadership. These books range in subject matter from ways to approach leadership to leadership in general. Some of them are now considered classics, while others have demonstrated new ways of studying leadership. One thing is certain, the study of leadership is continuous, and more than just the positive side of leadership is now being seriously studied, as will be seen later in this chapter.

1.2 THE STUDY OF LEADERSHIP IN LIBRARY AND INFORMATION STUDIES (LIS)

The statement that the study of leadership in the field of LIS has been minimal is not a surprise to any researcher in the field. Hernon (2007) propounds the notion that leadership literature in all research fields has exploded, with the exception of LIS. Even academic librarians, the practitioners of the field, know that not much research is being done in the field, though it has begun to improve slightly in the past five years. This lack of literature was addressed by Garson and Wallace (2014), "It is important that leaders recognize and employ library leadership literature that explicitly engages with the academic library's distinct organizational structure in theory and practice." This does not mean that management literature needs to stop, only that more research-based leadership literature needs to be published.

While I was researching the topic of leadership and academic libraries Mitchell's (1989) empirical study in an academic library surfaced. The journal article is about testing a contingency leadership theory in academic libraries. Assessment outcomes were preceded by a critique of the LIS literature that claimed that the limited discussions of leadership in the library literature were almost exclusively conceptual and a form of "armchair theorizing." Mitchell referenced a 1976 dissertation by Dragon that reviewed literature as far back as 1928. Dragon concluded, "When the topic [of leadership] does find its way into library literature, the result is often only the author's personal editorial on library administration with scant reference to the nature, function, and theories of leadership" (p. 43). Mitchell (1989) argued, however, that "libraries seem to be excellent places to study leadership"; he also noted that "libraries are complex organizations... consequently there may be a need for various leadership styles within the same organization" (p. 26). Unfortunately, the results of Mitchell's study suggested that contingency theories of leadership did not fit comfortably onto data about leadership in libraries. Mitchell, nevertheless, argued that more empirical studies are necessary.

While Dragon (1976) actually began her dissertation asserting, "leadership, although recognized by management theorists as an element in the management process, is generally neglected in the literature of library administration," she added, "Little is known about the leader behavior pattern of library administrators" (p. 1). Dragon's dissertation focused on the leadership behaviors of library administrators. She compared subordinates' written descriptions of their administrators with the administrators' own descriptions of what their duties were. Dragon saw her study as an initial effort. She concluded her dissertation by stating, "In order to educate future library administrators and to train or retrain incumbents, it is necessary to learn more about the nature and function of leadership as it exists in libraries" (p. 122).

Recently, a number of publications about leadership effectiveness and resiliency have appeared. These topics should perhaps be used as paths to explore and teach more meaningful leadership courses in LIS programs, or at least replace the basic management course most students take in the United States. Students would then become aware of this emerging body of literature in LIS, which happens to be firmly established in many other fields, such as business, education, and political science, to name a few. It must be recognized that more needs to be done to address the lack of leadership research in the field of LIS.

1.3 LEADERSHIP IN ACADEMIC LIBRARIES

Hernon and Rossiter (2007) declared in their book *Making a Difference: Leadership and Academic Libraries* that leadership in academic libraries is not a trend. It has now become a necessary function. As just noted, there is limited LIS literature focusing on leadership in general (Hernon, 2007; Hernon & Pors, 2013; Riggs, 1982, 2007). Owing to the dearth of research on leadership and the impact of leadership on academic libraries, no studies were found on the topic of toxic leadership in academic library settings.

An overwhelming majority of the academic librarians who participated in the research stated that successful leadership in academic libraries to them means leaders who trust them and treat them as the professional librarians they are; leaders who care about their libraries' place within the larger institution and advocate to make the library a better environment for everyone, not just themselves.

Librarians also like leaders who are humble, understanding, genuine, good communicators, competent, intelligent, visionary, strategic, empathetic, good listeners, hardworking, responsible, enthusiastic, team players, encouraging, caring, innovative, purposeful, confident, dedicated, receptive to input from librarians and staff, adaptable to the changing needs of academic libraries and higher education, and most importantly, prompt in decision making.

Ideally, academic library leaders are knowledgeable about librarianship, higher education, and its politics, and model positive leadership. They are also understanding of the library's needs and those of their librarians and staff needs and when applicable, good mentors. What these leaders are not: micromanagers, afraid to correct problems or problem employees, insecure, divisive, narcissistic, overbearing, inclined to pit librarians and staff against one another, vindictive, easily intimidated, or threatened by stellar librarians working under them, but these behaviors, as well as other significant ones, are yet to be reflected in the leadership literature with respect to academic libraries.

1.4 DEFINING TOXIC LEADERSHIP

From a review of a broad spectrum of the literature on destructive leadership and all of its subcategories (Craig & Kaiser (2013) claim that there are six: unethical leadership, abusive supervision, a dark/evil side of leadership, negligent/laissez-faire leadership, narcissistic leadership, and, especially, toxic leadership) written by the most frequently cited authors on the topic (i.e., Kellerman, 2004; Lipman-Blumen, 2005c; Pelletier, 2010; Reed & Olsen, 2010; Whicker, 1996), a definition of the term "toxic leadership" was developed for the study that preceded this book:

Toxic leadership requires egregious actions taken against some or all of the members, even among peers, of the organization a leader heads; actions that cause considerable and long-lasting damage to individuals and the organization that often continue even after the perpetrator has left the organization.

This definition was used to identify librarians in academic libraries who have experienced or witnessed toxic leadership in their work situations. Unlike Tepper's (2000) notion of abusive supervision, this definition accommodates the notion that a leader's dysfunctional behavior entails more than actions that occur in one-to-one relationships between supervisors and supervisees. It keeps open the possibility that a leader's or a co-worker's behavior can impact an entire organizational culture. Of course, the term toxic leadership also narrows the focus a little, because it excludes assumptions about sexual harassment or physical harm, which are normally explicitly covered by the terms destructive leadership and workplace violence.

There are a few additional aspects to my use of the term toxic leadership that should be noted here. First, this definition assumes that, once toxicity has spread throughout the whole organization, those who are able to do so may attempt to stop or at least slow down the behavior by appealing to a more senior administrator, while other employees will choose to be silent and remain neutral (Henley, 2003; Kellerman, 2004; Whicker, 1996). After exposing the toxic situation many employees can begin to focus again on their work and the mission of the organization. Also, once the situation has been acknowledged by a higher authority in the organization, those suffering from residual psychological and emotional damage may then contemplate seeking help to begin the healing process (Frost, 2003; Lubit, 2004; Kusy & Holloway, 2009). Those seeking help may include abused employees, witnesses, and whistle-blowers, among others. This definition is deliberately broad and should continue to evolve and solidify as more research on toxic leadership in academic libraries is undertaken.

1.5 IDENTIFYING TOXIC LEADERSHIP IN THE LITERATURE

Even though toxic leadership was described by Whicker (1996) and shown to have a damaging impact on the workplace, toxic leadership has evolved and is now associated with the broader destructive leadership construct. For Whicker (1996), a toxic leader possesses certain characteristics: deep-seated inadequacy, selfish values, and deceit, which become more apparent as the toxic environment spreads across an organization (p. 53). Defining destructive leadership, and particularly toxic leadership, however, continues to be an issue for some leadership scholars. Most researchers who study destructive leadership, or leadership in general, provide descriptions of behavior or impact that needs to be present to qualify the leader as destructive or toxic (Appelbaum & Roy-Girard, 2007; Craig & Kaiser, 2013; Kellerman, 2004; Lipman-Blumen, 2005a; Reed, 2004; Tepper, 2000). Examples of this approach are Lipman-Blumen (2005a), who declared that to define a toxic leader "we probably need a multidimensional framework, one that addresses their intentions, their behavior, their character, and the impact of the consequences of their decisions and actions" (p. 2). Reed (2004) wrote about the "toxic leader syndrome" which is identifiable by three key elements: (1) an apparent lack of concern for the well-being of subordinates, (2) a personality or interpersonal technique that negatively affects organizational climate, and (3) a conviction by subordinates that the leader is motivated primarily by self-interest (p. 67).

It can be said that toxic leadership in the workplace (be it corporate, non-profit, military, or whatever else) is demonstrated in myriad ways. Some abusive behaviors include humiliation, bullying, ridicule, belittling, telling employees publicly or privately that they are not part of the organization, ignoring, shunning, overworking, among many other forms of emotional and psychological abuse. Together, all of these experiences may cause loss of self-esteem, lack of pride in one's work, poorer quality of life, and loss of morale in the workplace (Kellerman, 2004; Pearson & Porath, 2005; Pelletier, 2010; Schyns & Schilling, 2013; Tepper, 2000; Tepper, 2007; Whicker, 1996). The toxic workplace has a leader that does not care for the well-being of employees or the organization, but cares only about him- or herself (Craig & Kaiser, 2013; Kellerman, 2004;

Lipman-Blumen, 2005a; Lipman-Blumen, 2005c; Reed, 2004; Whicker, 1996).

Presently, there is still a difference of opinions among researchers about how to identify a toxic leader. Padilla, Hogan, and Kaiser (2007) propose that it is the consequences that identify a toxic leader, while accepting that many other researchers in the field believe it to be more than outcomes and include the leaders' behaviors and their treatment of their employees (Craig & Kaiser, 2013; Kusy & Holloway, 2009; Lipman-Blumen, 2005a; Reed, 2004; Reed & Olsen, 2010). Padilla et al. (2007) propose a toxic triangle that must be present to create a destructive environment with catastrophic consequences—a destructive charismatic leader, susceptible followers, and facilitative environments (p. 179). While, Krasikova, Green, and LeBreton (2013) propose that all that is needed for a situation to be characterized as toxic is a destructive leader who, with deliberate intention, displays damaging behavior intended to hurt an organization and/or his or her followers by pushing personal agendas that damage the organization's well-being. Such leaders may also lead by using hurtful methods of influence with weak justifications in order to reach their preferred ends.

Even if it is usually leaders along with their managers who create and allow the toxic behavior to take place, followers can also play a significant role in the creation of a toxic environment. According to Ortega, Hogh, Pejtersen, and Olsen (2009) workplace bullying (another term related to toxic leadership) is reflected in the literature as being carried out by both supervisors and co-workers. Their study also showed that this behavior occurs more readily in professions with a high gender ratio, regardless of whether they are characteristically feminine (e.g., nursing, education, and librarianship) or masculine professions (e.g., engineering, military, and politics). Hence, supervisors who may have established toxic workplaces through their actions, are probably in some instances creating subordinates who erroneously believe that they too can treat their colleagues in a hostile manner. Hogh and Dofradottir's (2001) study, unlike Ortega et al.'s (2009) study, found that co-workers were most frequently reported as the perpetrators of ill treatment in the workplace. Thus, even when working in a so-called flat or low power distance organization (Ortega et al., 2009) there are always differences among co-workers, such as seniority, or simply the fact that one may just happen to be working closely with the manager. Regardless of the co-workers' relationships, hierarchies are inevitably established, even if informally, potentially leading to peer-to-peer incivility or lateral/horizontal violence (Dellasega, 2011; Kaminski & Sincox, 2012; Kaucher, 2014).

Subordinates who are abused are in many cases left feeling unappreciated and might not want to work to their full potential under such toxic conditions. Those who wish to rise above toxic situations, past and present, may need to learn how to identify such individuals, in the case that their organization is full of toxic people, who negatively affect the organization as a whole, even after the original toxic leader has departed (Appelbaum & Roy-Girard, 2007; Kellerman, 2004; Kusy & Holloway, 2009; Lipman–Blumen, 2005b; Reed, 2004; Staninger, 2012; Walton, 2007; Whicker, 1996).

Special attention is given in the literature to the role followers play in a toxic leader's environment. The role of followers clearly needs further exploration (Craig & Kaiser, 2013; Kellerman, 2004; Lipman–Blumen, 2005a; Padilla et al., 2007). However, the main focus of this book is toxic leadership and its impact on an academic library rather than on how followers contribute to a toxic environment. Yet, it is important to acknowledge that leaders and followers work together, because "Without followers nothing happens including bad leadership" (Kellerman, 2004, p. 226).

The literature overview also noted that toxic leadership is not reserved for subordinates; even upper management can be intimidated. But that does not mean they will run away from their jobs; a sense of duty and enjoyment of their jobs help to keep them going to work (Reed & Bullis, 2009). Regardless of the position of the targeted person, the option of staying is much easier when the person attacked has some power within the organizational structure. To summarize, toxic leadership can be seen as part of organizational life at every level in the hierarchy of an organization (Lubit, 2004; Kusy & Holloway, 2009).

1.6 TOXIC LEADERSHIP IN ACADEMIC LIBRARIES

As noted already, there is limited LIS literature focusing on leadership (Hernon, 2007; Hernon & Pors, 2013; Riggs, 1982; Riggs, 2007). Consequently, it is not surprising that there is even less research on ineffective or problematic leadership in academic libraries. To date there are "no studies [that] have explored leader errors and how such errors influence organizational success" (Hernon & Pors, 2013, p. 200) in what little there is about positive leadership.

A comprehensive search effort for academic literature about toxic leadership in academic libraries began with searches in the LIS literature. The LISA (Library and Information Science Abstracts), LISTA (Library, Information Science & Technology Abstracts), and Library Literature & Information Science Full Text databases were searched because this is where most of the literature on all aspects of academic libraries resides. Databases[1] that cover leadership and management topics were also used.

Very few articles dealing with *academic libraries* and *management* in general were found. It was even more difficult to find articles dealing with toxic leadership in academic libraries. Only a few of the articles that came up were somewhat related to the topic. These scarce results demonstrate that even if toxic leadership is already present in academic libraries and has been informally spoken about, it has not been recognized in the field sufficiently to be formally studied and published.

The literature generated during extensive searching for literature about—or at least related to—toxic leadership, was limited in pertinence. Only one of the two papers, i.e., Proctor (2001), explicitly mentioned that leaders in public libraries can be destructive. One other paper labeled the leader as ineffective (Staninger, 2012); a third suggested that a highly stressful workplace can lead to a toxic environment (Siamian, Shahrabi, Vahedi, Abbsai Rad, & Cherati, 2006).

The articles found in the search for LIS literature on toxic leadership suggest that some library personnel feel demoralized, undervalued, and/or stressed (Proctor, 2001; Siamian et al., 2006; Staninger, 2012) when there is a lack of effective leadership. Some of these articles also discussed the values and ethics that were needed for a leader to be effective, but this aspect, more often than not, was addressed using a business ethics lens, even though that perspective is not typically employed in examining the field of LIS (Barsh & Lisewski, 2009; Schachter, 2008). Some of the articles also mentioned how little is known about leadership in library contexts; even less has been written about ineffective and bad leadership in academic libraries (Riggs, 2007).

Unfortunately, the sparse results suggest that little learning about toxic leadership based on formal empirical studies exists. There is a lack of robust systematic empirical research in the LIS field regarding the situations in which some academic librarians work. The literature as a whole

---

[1] Business Source Premier, Dissertations and Theses Full Text, Education Source, Emerald, JStor, Lexis-Nexis Academic Universe, PsycINFO, Sage Premier Journals, Web of Knowledge, as well as Google Scholar.

only acknowledges that destructive leadership is sometimes present in libraries, and does not clearly document the occurrence, at times, of toxic leadership in academic libraries. Of all the articles that have emerged, only one includes the word "toxic" (Ghosh, 2006). The preferred terms found in this review of the research thus far have been "ineffective" or "unethical" leadership.

To summarize, to date there has been a limited quantity of research focusing on leadership in libraries, and even less on toxic leadership. The work that has been done has not often been grounded in systematic empirical research. Since 2011, listserv activity indicates an increase in efforts to improve leadership in libraries through calls and invitations to participate in library leadership institutes, such as the American Library Association's Leadership Institute, and discussion groups (e.g., Association of College and Research Libraries — Leadership Discussion Group).

These calls support Riggs's prediction that:

We are witnessing some approaches that will strengthen library leadership (e.g., institutes and senior fellow programs), and more emphasis on development of library leaders is yet to come. Making ineffective library leaders more effective will improve current and future services of libraries (2007, p. 187–188).

This search of the literature in LIS demonstrated that the topic of toxic leadership in libraries is not yet being seriously pursued as a research subject, nor is it included in research about academic libraries. However, a growing interest in discussions about library leadership via listservs and library leadership institutes organized by academic library associations suggests that there is a potential audience for this book. This book adds to the discussion on leadership in academic libraries that is in development, mostly outside of the realm of LIS, and rather in librarians' professional organizations and leadership studies fora.

REFERENCES

Appelbaum, S. H., & Roy-Girard, D. (2007). Toxins in the workplace: Affect on organizations and employees. *Corporate Governance, 7*(1), 17–28.

Barsh, A., & Lisewski, A. (2009). Library managers and ethical leadership: A survey of current practices from the perspective of business ethics. In A. L. Besnoy (Ed.), *Ethics and integrity in libraries* (pp. 57–65). New York, NY: Routledge.

Burns, J. M. (1978). *Leadership.* New York, NY: Harper & Row.

Craig, S. B., & Kaiser, R. B. (2013). Destructive leadership. In M. G. Rumsey (Ed.), *Oxford handbook of leadership* (pp. 439–454). Oxford: Oxford University Press.

Dellasega, C. (2011). *When nurses hurt nurses: Recognizing and overcoming the cycle of bullying.* Indianapolis, IN: Sigma Theta Tau International.

Dragon, A.C. (1976). Self-descriptions and subordinate descriptions of the leader behavior of library administrators. (Order No. 7712796, University of Minnesota). ProQuest Dissertations and Theses. Retrieved from <http://0-search.proquest.com.sally.sandiego.edu/docview/302804727?accountid=14742>.

Fiedler, F. E., & Chemers, M. (1984). *Improving leadership effectiveness*. New York, NY: John Wiley.

Frost, P. J. (2003). *Toxic emotions at work: How compassionate managers handle pain and conflict*. Boston, MA: Harvard Business School Press.

Garson, D. S., & Wallace, D. (2014). Leadership capabilities in the midst of transition at the Harvard Library. In B. L. Eden, & J. C. Fagan (Eds.), *Leadership in academic libraries today: Connecting theory to practice* (pp. 41−74). Lanham, MD: Rowman & Littlefield.

Ghosh, M. (2006). ALIEP-2006 conference on library leadership at Nanyang Technological University, Singapore: A summary report. Retrieved from <http://eprints.rclis.org/8128/1/ALIEP__leadership.pdf>.

Henley, K. (2003). Detoxifying a toxic leader. *Innovative leader, 12*(6). Retrieved from <http://www.winstonbrill.com/bril001/html/article_index/articles/551-600/article578_body.html>.

Hernon, P. (2007). The LIS leadership literature. In P. Hernon, & N. Rossiter (Eds.), *Making a difference: Leadership and academic libraries* (pp. 61−68). Westport, CT: Libraries Unlimited.

Hernon, P., & Pors, N. O. (2013). Leadership as viewed across countries. In P. Hernon, & N. O. Pors (Eds.), *Library leadership in the United States and Europe: Comparative study of academic and public libraries* (pp. 191−204). Santa Barbara, CA: Libraries Unlimited.

Hernon, P., & Rossiter, N. (Eds.), (2007). *Making a difference: Leadership and academic libraries* Westport, CT: Libraries Unlimited.

Hogh, A., & Dofradottir, A. (2001). Coping with bullying in the workplace. *European Journal of Work and Organizational Psychology, 10*(4), 485−495.

Kaminski, M., & Sincox, A.K. (2012). *Workplace bullying in health care: Peer-to-peer bullying of nurses*. Retrieved from <http://ilera2012.wharton.upenn.edu/RefereedPapers/KaminskiMichelle.pdf>.

Kaucher, A.C. (2014). *Lived experiences of registered nurses in relation to horizontal violence in the workplace*. ProQuest Dissertations & Theses Full Text, Thesis.

Kellerman, B. (2004). *Bad leadership: What it is, how it happens, why it matters*. Boston, MA: Harvard Business School Press.

Krasikova, D. V., Green, S. G., & LeBreton, J. M. (2013). Destructive leadership: A theoretical review, integration, and future research agenda. *Journal of Management, Advance online publication*, 1−31. Available from http://dx.doi.org/10.1177/0149206312471388, January 25, 2013.

Kusy, M. E., & Holloway, E. L. (2009). *Toxic workplace!: Managing toxic personalities and their systems of power*. San Francisco CA: Jossey-Bass.

Lipman-Blumen, J. (2005a). The allure of toxic leaders: Why followers rarely escape their clutches. *Ivey Business Journal, 69*(3), 1−8.

Lipman-Blumen, J. (2005b). Toxic leadership: When grand illusions masquerade as noble visions. *Leader to Leader, 2005*(36), 29−36. Available from http://dx.doi.org/10.1002/ltl.125.

Lipman-Blumen, J. (2005c). *The allure of toxic leaders: Why we follow destructive bosses and corrupt politicians—and how we can survive them*. Oxford: Oxford University Press.

Lubit, R. H. (2004). *Coping with toxic managers, subordinates -and other difficult people*. Upper Saddle River, NJ: FT Prentice Hall.

Mavranic, M. A. (2005). Transformation leadership: Peer mentoring as a values-based learning process. *Portal: Libraries and the Academy, 5*(3), 391−404.

Mitchell, E. (1989). The library leadership project: A test of leadership effectiveness in academic libraries. *Advances in Library Administration and Organization, 8*, 25—38.

Ortega, A., Hogh, A., Pejtersen, J. H., & Olsen, O. (2009). Prevalence of workplace bullying and risk groups: A representative population study. *International Archives of Occupational and Environmental Health, 82*, 417—426. Available from http://dx.doi.org/10.1007/s00420-008-0339-8.

Padilla, A., Hogan, R., & Kaiser, R. B. (2007). The toxic triangle: Destructive leaders, susceptible followers, and conducive environments. *The Leadership Quarterly, 18*, 176—194.

Pearson, C. M., & Porath, C. L. (2005). On the nature, consequences and remedies of workplace incivility: No time for "Nice"? Think again. *Academy of Management Executive, 19*(1), 7—18.

Pelletier, K. L. (2010). Leader toxicity: An empirical investigation of toxic behavior and rhetoric. *Leadership, 6*(4), 373—389.

Proctor, R. (2001). A personnel time bomb. *Public Library Journal, 16*(3), 69—70.

Reed, G. E. (2004). Toxic leadership. *Military Review, 84*(4), 67—71.

Reed, G. E., & Bullis, R. C. (2009). The impact of destructive leadership on senior military officers and civilian employees. *Armed Forces & Society, 36*(1), 5—18.

Reed, G. E., & Olsen, R. A. (2010). Toxic leadership: Part deux. *Military Review, 90*(6), 58—64.

Riggs, D. E. (Ed.), (1982). *Library leadership: Visualizing the future* Phoenix, Az: Oryx Press.

Riggs, D. E. (2001). The crisis and opportunity in library leadership. *Journal of Library Administration, 32*(3/4), 5—17.

Riggs, D. E. (2007). Ineffective [bad!] Leadership. In P. Hernon, & N. Rossiter (Eds.), *Making a difference: Leadership and academic libraries* (pp. 181—188). Westport, CT: Libraries Unlimited.

Schachter, D. (2008). Learn to embrace opposition for improved decision making. *Information Outlook, 12*(10), 44—45.

Schyns, B., & Schilling, J. (2013). How bad are the effects of bad leaders? A meta-analysis of destructive leadership and its outcomes. *The Leadership Quarterly, 24*, 138—158.

Siamian, H., Shahrabi, A., Vahedi, M., Abbsai Rad, A. M., & Cherati, J. Y. (2006). Stress and burnout in libraries & information centers. In C. Khoo, D. Singh, & A. S. Chaudhry (Eds.), *Proceedings of the Asia-Pacific conference on library & information education & practice 2006 (A-LIEP 2006)* (pp. 263—268). Singapore: Singapore: School of Communication & Information, Nanyang Technological University.

Staninger, S. W. (2012). Identifying the presence of ineffective leadership in libraries. *Library Leadership & Management, 26*(1), 1—7.

Tepper, B. J. (2000). Consequences of abusive supervision. *Academy of Management Journal, 43*(2), 178—190.

Tepper, B. J. (2007). Abusive supervision in work organizations: Review, synthesis, and research agenda. *Journal of Management, 33*(3), 261—289.

Walton, M. (2007). Leadership toxicity: An inevitable affliction of organisations? *Organizations & People, 14*(1), 19—27.

Whicker, M. L. (1996). *Toxic leaders: When organizations go bad*. Westport, CT: Quorum Books.

CHAPTER 2

How to Acknowledge Toxic Leadership's Presence

Recognizing that there is a problem in an academic library can take some time. First comes disbelief, and then denial. These two behaviors are the first steps to realizing that things are not going as well as librarians thought. Then, other librarians who also recognize the uncivilized behavior have to be found, otherwise there is the risk that the victimized librarians may turn toward disbelief, or worse, wonder if it is all in their heads and begin to ask if they could possibly be going crazy or are maybe simply having a rough day, week, or month at work.

At first it may seem as if it was an isolated incident, or that the academic librarians are always excusing what just happened. Later on, after a clear pattern has emerged, it is time for librarians to take action for themselves. They may by then have acknowledged the magnitude of the problem existing in their library, but they may still be alone and wondering if others see it too. Librarians may begin to ask themselves, is there only one toxic leader, or are there toxic leaders? Are they only *after* a few librarians, or a specific group of librarians? Maybe only one librarian in particular is being persecuted, on account of her or his activities in the library, such as demanding innovation, or other improvements that would shake the status quo?

Acknowledging the presence of a toxic leader is not always an easy process, in fact it usually is not. This is especially true if only some of the librarians see what is happening, while others do not, and there are also the others, librarians who may be in on it with the toxic leader and are enacting the leader's wishes. This is a lot to accept rationally, and much more difficult to accept all at once as occurring in the library. Reconciling everything that is happening all at once will take time.

Are some librarians being overworked, belittled, verbally abused, bullied, mobbed, shunned, backbitten, gossiped about, threatened, or having their ideas stolen by peers or supervisors, or even getting stressed out over work done supposedly incorrectly, although they performed the task to the supervisor specifications provided? Toxic behaviors are not

Academic Libraries and Toxic Leadership.
DOI: http://dx.doi.org/10.1016/B978-0-08-100637-5.00002-9

always overt. They can be hidden in plain view or caught at the moment least expected. For example, a librarian comes out of a meeting visibly upset or crying and when asked if everything is all right, replies that yes, everything is fine. Victimized librarians most likely do not want to draw attention to themselves out of fear. Their supervisor could become even more upset with them. Observing that peers become suddenly distant and participate less in work-related social events or it may be that the observing librarians are the ones who actually distanced themselves from their colleagues, these are signs of a potential toxic leader at play.

Another very common toxic behavior at meetings occurs when a librarian, typically a woman, shares her ideas or opinions openly, only to have them ignored or "not heard" by the group, and then, minutes later, someone else repeats almost exactly or verbatim what the ignored librarian said and is congratulated and given credit for presenting such a great idea. If this behavior is ongoing and is happening to only a certain librarian or subgroup of librarians, then toxic leadership is at hand. When the leaders of departments, committees, or libraries see this happening and do nothing to stop it, then they are actively participating in the mobbing. The leaders' favorite librarians are usually the ones who benefit from the seizing of ideas and projects that are not their own. If the librarian who was wronged complains to the leader and the leader says that the wronged librarian needs to be more collaborative and less envious of his or her peers' accomplishments and if incidents like this have happened more than twice, it should be realized that this leader is in on it, whether the leader is cognizant of his or her actions or not.

2.1 THE EFFECTS OF TOXIC LEADERSHIP

Before taking action against toxic leadership it is important to know its impact or effect on an organization and its employees. Toxic leadership is harmful in a variety of ways at different levels within the organization, including the academic library.

Much of the literature mentions that toxic leadership has an impact not just on the workplace, but also on the employees, in ways that extend beyond the boundaries of the workplace (Craig & Kaiser, 2013; Henley, 2003; Kaminski & Sincox, 2012; Kellerman, 2004; Lipman-Blumen, 2005a; Porath & Pearson, 2005, 2013; Tepper, 2000; Whicker, 1996). Regrettably the academic library is no exception, as will be seen later on in this chapter.

Lipman-Blumen (2005a) proclaimed that "most whistle-blowers encounter grave risks to careers, families and fortunes" (p. 8). Henley (2003) and Lipman-Blumen (2005a) raise the importance of recognizing the existence of "toxin handlers," i.e., those employees in the organization who help the organization move forward by their dedication while also helping enclose the toxicity. Toxin handlers play an important role in sustaining the organization, but they also hope that the current situation will not persist for a long time because it is not bearable for long periods of time (Appelbaum & Roy-Girard, 2007; Frost, 2003). Toxin handlers, although they are needed buffers for the organization, also need help because they can succumb to the toxic environment themselves, which can take them to the point of burnout or illness (Frost, 2003).

Toxic behaviors represent a problem in higher education, including academic libraries, because they negatively impact retention, morale, and productivity, and they can result in a hostile work environment (Klein & Lester, 2013). In a toxic environment, anyone working in the organization is in a position to observe toxic exchanges in a way that negatively impacts service provision and reputation (Porath, MacInnis, & Folkes, 2010). Holmes (2001) proclaimed that "excessive stress is … destructive leading to a deterioration in performance as well as job dissatisfaction, accidents, unsafe working practices and high absenteeism" (p. 230). These behaviors brought on by high stress would undoubtedly impact an organization's services, as well as making for poor collegial relationships, leading to a change in their output of organizational citizenship behaviors, in some instances leading to something very similar to Post Traumatic Stress Disorder (PTSD) and other health problems as work conditions deteriorate (Coyne, 2011; Frost, 2003; Kaminski & Sincox, 2012; Kusy & Holloway, 2009; Organ, 1997; Sutton, 2010). If team members are not getting along well, owing to high stress and turnover, there is a possibility that some individuals on the team will also engage in what Holmes (2001, p. 231) called "escape strategies," such as absenteeism to cope, because high turnover in many instances results in staff having to take on additional responsibilities until qualified personnel are hired to fill the open positions.

Holmes (2001) also affirmed that "job dissatisfaction, whatever the cause, is clearly detrimental to any organisation's aims and objectives making it difficult to meet organisational and/or departmental goals" (p. 231). These behaviors become financially costly to the library's administration, as eventually new staff will need to be hired and trained to maintain a minimum level of client services (Kusy & Holloway, 2009).

The costs of reduced work effort due to toxic leadership are far more than monetary. Besides loss of profit, organizations could also see their reputation affected and employees may begin to show low morale, burnout, and anxiety, and in some instances may begin to consider other work options (Coyne, 2011; Forni, 2008; Frost, 2003; Holloway & Kusy, 2010; Kusy & Holloway, 2009; Lubit, 2004; Pearson & Porath, 2005; Porath & Pearson, 2013; Rose, Shuck, Twyford, & Bergman, 2015; Sutton 2010; Tepper, 2000).

Toxic leadership's impact is so strong that "research has shown that individuals can be harmed by merely being exposed to, hearing about, or witnessing toxic and dysfunctional workplace behavior" (Lemmergaard & Muhr, 2013, p. 16). This is why it is of the utmost importance to have a way to counter it once it has manifested in an organization, especially in academic libraries, which are highly social and integral parts of universities, colleges, and research centers.

2.2 EFFECTS ON ACADEMIC LIBRARIANS

At first effects may not be visible to anyone but the librarian being singled out by the toxic supervisor. Yet, as the toxicity permeates the entire library, its effects inevitably become palpable. Although not necessarily immediate, the effects are many, from loss of morale through a stoppage in user services to affecting librarians' own professional output. More than half of the interviewed academic librarians said that their personal lives suffered. However, at the beginning of the abuse these effects may not be obvious to anyone, including the victimized librarian. The symptoms of toxic leadership are varied and on many occasions these are attributed to other aspects of the librarian's life.

The top two effects academic librarians reported were becoming demoralized and experiencing a decline in productivity. They lost trust in their leader and some of their peers. In many instances, academic librarians felt undermined and that their hard work was not appreciated, which led to a loss of confidence in their work. Toxic leadership and the associated abuse in academic libraries is not a recent phenomenon, but has been going on for a long time and has been labeled a variety of things, ranging from rudeness through workplace incivility, insidious workplace behavior, to mobbing, to plain toxic leadership. Regardless of what it is called, it has effects on the quality of librarians' work life.

Nevertheless, many academic librarians have dealt with toxic leaders by becoming the best librarians they could be. Many became published authors, whereas others sought more professional development opportunities in their respective fields, such as presentations and teaching engagements, preferably outside of the institution. These professional activities allowed for a mental respite from their toxic libraries. Eventually, however, services suffered because the once contented librarians, eager to do their jobs, no longer felt the same commitment toward their work. These feelings are difficult to reconcile for many academic librarians because they consider themselves to be hardworking and/or passionate about their work. They pride themselves on putting in their best effort. Their organizational citizenship behavior inevitably decreased; in other words, they no longer felt appreciated, they felt burned-out from doing other librarians' work due to high turnover, or worse, because they were deliberately being overworked by their toxic leaders.

So many people left, everyone did two to three jobs for about three years. We're so overworked. There's mental and physical burnout, low morale, and we don't trust the process anymore.

There have been instances where, as one librarian was developing coping mechanisms for dealing with the toxic environment, another librarian in another department was starting to deal with how this could be happening to him or her. These librarians are ambivalent about who to reach out to with their dilemma and suffer in silence for months or years.

In some academic libraries user services programming has stopped because the librarians who were able to leave the toxic environment left, and thus the remaining librarians were left to carry on not only with their own duties, but also those of the librarians who have quit.

Nonetheless, there were a few librarians, very few, two in fact, who were able to completely compartmentalize and separate their work situations from their personal lives. These librarians claimed to have succeeded in preventing the toxic environment from affecting them outside of the library. They stated that they were fortunate in having strong family networks living nearby, and selected a mentor or co-worker in whom they could confide about their work situation. They also credited their unscathed survival to leading full lives outside of work. Their library career, although valued, was not more important than the other parts of their lives.

There's this toxic cloud, you go in, you have to breathe the fumes in...You have to be very conscious about the boundaries you put up, so that you don't unintentionally and against your will breathe in more than you really want to.

Librarians who worked under toxic leadership conditions for an extended period of time felt they had diminished their human capacity.

Work cannot and should not be everything to librarians, because toxic leaders will abuse their dedication. These dedicated librarians will in due course burn out and their toxic leaders will not care about their happiness at work, because to them, everyone is expendable. Work-focused lives seem to have in some cases unintentionally assisted toxic leaders with their exploitative behaviors.

Table 2.1 Most Common Toxic Leadership Effects on Academic Librarians

In the words of librarians:
- Really low morale, fear, and absolute capitulation of your potential. You just shut down. People don't do much, there's a revolving door. I began to consciously edit and censor my behavior to fit into her rules for her to be nice to me.
- Our library morale is the lowest since the past 40 years. Fortunately, she was forced to step down to do a librarian's job and has been out of our library as of July 2015.
- Toxic leadership makes it incredibly unpleasant to be at work. It causes me to question my own abilities, and my perceptions of situations. It makes me feel as though my work is not valued, or I'm not doing things right. It becomes difficult to approach the "leader" with new ideas or feedback. It increases my level of anxiety - to the extent of occasional panic attacks when anticipating interaction with the "leader."
- People literally fell ill due to the stress of working under him. People have retired early to get away from him. People with decades of work experience at this institution have left for other institutions to escape him (turnover).
- Recently, yelling and incivility slowed my progress down significantly. One doesn't feel like pouring all one's energy into work when punishment is harsh and arbitrary. It makes it seem as though one has no control over one's work / fate /reputation / competence. It is the preferred leadership style in the institution where I still work.
- For years we had the devil as our leader. It was terrible. People were scared of her. Meetings were torturous. There were absences, a lot of distrust, shouting matches. . . This woman created rifts and pitted people against each other.
- I stopped doing my best. I stopped giving my potential because I knew that that would put me in trouble. That's not appropriate but that's how it was. I tried to find simple things to keep busy and did not try to pursue anything that could ruffle any feathers. I was responding this way to survive. Collectively what resulted was a stagnant, low performing, non-innovative place where everyone's just a little siloed and doing the minimal to survive, that's it.
- It's exhausting to keep boundaries in order to survive. It's not only exhausting it's depressing and demoralizing.
- I dreaded going into work each day and began taking medication for anxiety and insomnia. All that evaporated the day she was terminated. It took us literally years to recover an organizational climate where people felt secure and confident in voicing their opinions.

Source: Ortega (2015).

The effects of toxic leadership on academic libraries and librarians are many, Table 2.1 captures the most commonly reported effects of toxic leadership on academic librarians, which ranged from affecting their personal output to feeling undermined and unappreciated for their hard work and dedication.

2.3 EFFECTS ON USER SERVICES

It is only when the situation at an academic library has deteriorated so much that members of the university community—students, faculty, staff, and administration, notice the toxic interactions between librarians or the loss of services that begins to impact the whole university. Once this happens, the library's reputation has been tarnished and it can even give the institution a bad name. Only a toxic leader who is self-involved allows the library's productivity and services to degenerate. Loss of services and of a productive work environment undoubtedly impact users' perception of the library.

It takes time for the library to be accepted again as a place where students can study, professors do research, and all of them receive great services and comfortably access library resources. Once the problem is disclosed, it is important not to hide what is happening in the library. It is in fact the inaction (which is indeed a type of action) that allows many academic librarians to suffer in silence, because no one outside the library notices the duress they are under. It also does not help that to many in upper administration librarians themselves are invisible. And it does not matter whether the academic librarians are classified as faculty, administrators, or staff. Libraries in academic institutions are simply seen as an academic service, while the people working in them are unappreciated. Toxic leaders advocate for themselves, not their library or their librarians.

Besides the fact that most people working in higher education settings are not trained to recognize the toxic leadership types of behavior, aside of course from the student counselors, who are trained to identify not only mental illness, but also high stress, compulsive behaviors, and fear, among other indicators of mental abuse happening to students. It should be noted that it is only within the past decade that university-sanctioned online trainings have emerged in higher education institutions all over the United States. These online trainings vary from learning what to do in an active shooter situation, through how to identify sexual harassment, to helping students with psychological difficulties. But to date there are no trainings on how to identify a toxic leader (or peer) in the academic workplace.

Ultimately, it is academic librarians who create and deliver services to users. If users are impacted in a negative way, such as in the reduction of services (workshops, hours, research consultations, etc.), not meeting users' needs, and not innovating or keeping up with technological advances, the library's reputation will be tainted.

High turnover also has an effect on user services, with the unintended consequence of overworking the remaining librarians. Users will certainly notice their favorite librarian is no longer there or that their favorite workshops have been canceled indefinitely. To the best of their ability librarians must take care to impact user services minimally; however, this may not always be possible. One very respected and well-liked librarian quit the day before final examinations began, intending to send a message to the library dean. The dean was extremely toxic, therefore the only people hurt, because of the last-minute cancellation of workshops were the students. The librarian, who left for a position at another university, loved her work, but she knew she had to leave because after 4 years of relentless abuse she could no longer cope; and so she ended up turning on her own liaison students.

The only way in which having users notice that things are not quite right in the library could be useful is if users report their concerns about changing attitudes in the library or its services to university personnel outside of the library, and do not inadvertently report this to the toxic leader. Realistically, this is more likely possible for faculty, administrators, and staff who are supportive of the library than it is for students, who are coming into and leaving the higher education institution every year. Administrators, faculty, and staff, if things are going well in their units, will and should be around much longer, making them ideal to take an active interest in the campus library.

2.4 WHEN IS IT NOT TOXIC LEADERSHIP?

As mentioned in the previous chapter, toxic leadership includes egregious actions of any kind including, but is not limited to: demeaning, shunning, ignoring, bullying, mobbing, gas-lighting, overworking, backbiting, berating, among others. Librarians must remain vigilant to see if these behaviors are happening to any of their colleagues or themselves. Sometimes it can be confusing to figure out if a supervisor is actually a toxic leader, Table 2.2 attempts to clarify what some librarians

Table 2.2 When is it NOT Toxic Leadership?

Scenarios of non toxic leadership but which could come across as such:

- If the library dean or department supervisors are dynamic and have high, and even more than reasonable, expectations of their librarians, it is not toxic leadership. These leaders are just making librarians cognizant of the realistic expectations they have for them. After all, librarians were hired to perform specific librarian duties. Ideally, these leaders are not manifesting unrealistic expectations of their librarians.
- When a leader possesses a "self-starter" attitude, values discipline, and sets realistic deadlines for his or her staff, this leader's skill sets should not be confused with toxic leadership. It is important to remember that toxic leaders care only about themselves and not the library or its librarians. The narcissistic tendencies of true toxic leaders are revealed when they declare candidly that their needs come first regardless, of any urgent needs the library has.
- For diverse reasons leaders may be absent. At smaller institutions library directors often serve on many types of committees, which inevitably take them away from the library. Other times they leave for conferences, if they are still active in professional associations. As long as the library has active department heads, and one is left in charge and things are running smoothly, there is no reason to accuse the library director of toxic leadership. But if the leader regularly disappears and does not openly communicate with librarians about who is in charge while he/she is away, to make decisions and resolve problems, then the lack of communication and absent leadership becomes problematic and could be on its way to becoming toxic leadership.
- When librarians are not fulfilling their responsibilities and transparency is being asked of them by their leaders that is not toxic leadership. Librarians may be annoyed by all of their responsibilities, but that does not mean their leaders should be vilified to others on campus or outside the institution. It is most probable that the leader merely wants to know how projects are progressing. Librarians should be comfortable in this give and take of academic work life and talk about workloads and if they feel they are close to being overworked.
- Everyone has a different personality and being sensitive does not give librarians the right to denounce a library leader as toxic simply because he/she happened to make some librarians feel badly about themselves or something they did. If the leader is mercurial, that is one issue that will definitely need to be addressed, but if it is all about personalities clashing, then both the leader and the librarian will need to work on their interactions with each other.
- Incompetence in a leader does not necessarily make for a toxic leader. The leader can learn to be better at his/her job if they have the desire. Some librarians, though, have seen the Peter Principle at work for too long and now see it coupled with toxic leadership leading to disaster for libraries. In essence, incompetence is onerous, not toxic.

erroneously perceived to be toxic leadership. These scenarios came up multiple times while conducting the librarian interviews.

Of course, all that has been listed in the table does not mean librarians have to ignore obvious toxic leadership behaviors, much less patterns, if these clearly emerge. If toxic leadership is happening in your library it must be reported. However, it is important to distinguish when it is not toxic leadership to avoid unnecessary confusion and needlessly lose credibility within the institution. Librarians who make accusations without merit ultimately hurt not only themselves, but also the library in the eyes of the institution's upper administration.

REFERENCES

Appelbaum, S. H., & Roy-Girard, D. (2007). Toxins in the workplace: Affect on organizations and employees. *Corporate Governance*, 7(1), 17−28.

Coyne, I. (2011). Bullying in the workplace. In C. P. Monks, & I. Coyne (Eds.), *Bullying in different contexts* (pp. 157−184). New York, NY: Cambridge University Press.

Craig, S. B., & Kaiser, R. B. (2013). Destructive leadership. In M. G. Rumsey (Ed.), *Oxford handbook of leadership* (pp. 439−454). Oxford: Oxford University Press.

Forni, P. M. (2008). *The civility solution: What to do when people are rude.* New York, NY: St. Martin's Griffin.

Frost, P. J. (2003). *Toxic emotions at work: How compassionate managers handle pain and conflict.* Boston, MA: Harvard Business School Press.

Henley, K. (2003). Detoxifying a toxic leader. *Innovative Leader*, 12(6). Retrieved from http://www.winstonbrill.com/bril001/html/article_index/articles/551-600/article578_body.html.

Holloway, E. L., & Kusy, M. E. (2010). Disruptive and toxic behaviors in healthcare: Zero tolerance, the bottom line and what to do about it. *Medical Practice Management*, 334−340, May/June.

Holmes, S. (2001). Work-related stress: A brief review. *Journal of the Royal Society for the Promotion of Health*, 121(4), 230−235.

Kaminski, M., & Sincox, A.K. (2012). *Workplace bullying in health care: Peer-to-peer bullying of nurses.* Retrieved from <http://ilera2012.wharton.upenn.edu/RefereedPapers/KaminskiMichelle.pdf>.

Kellerman, B. (2004). *Bad leadership: What it is, how it happens, why it matters.* Boston, MA: Harvard Business School Press.

Klein, C., & Lester, J. (2013). Moving beyond awareness and tolerance: Recommendations and implications for workplace bullying in higher education. In J. Lester (Ed.), *Workplace bullying in higher education* (pp. 138−147). New York, NY: Routledge.

Kusy, M. E., & Holloway, E. L. (2009). *Toxic workplace!: Managing toxic personalities and their systems of power.* San Francisco, CA: Jossey-Bass.

Lemmergaard, J., & Muhr, S. L. (2013). Broadening the critical leadership repertoire: Emotions, toxicity and dysfunctionality. In J. Lemmergaard, & S. L. Muhr (Eds.), *Critical perspectives on leadership: Emotion, toxicity and dysfunction* (pp. 3−26). Northampton, MA: Edward Elgar.

Lipman-Blumen, J. (2005a). The allure of toxic leaders: Why followers rarely escape their clutches. *Ivey Business Journal*, 69(3), 1−8.

Lubit, R. H. (2004). *Coping with toxic managers, subordinates—and other difficult people.* Upper Saddle River, NJ: FT Prentice Hall.

Organ, D. W. (1997). Organizational citizenship behavior: It's construct clean-up time. *Human Performance*, *10*(2), 85–97.

Ortega, A. (2015). Leadership Styles in Academic Libraries Survey.

Pearson, C. M., & Porath, C. L. (2005). On the nature, consequences and remedies of workplace incivility: No time for "Nice"? Think again. *Academy of Management Executive*, *19*(1), 7–18.

Porath, C., MacInnis, D., & Folkes, V. (2010). Witnessing incivility among employees: Effects on consumer anger and negative inferences about companies. *Journal of Consumer Research*, *37*, 292–303.

Porath, C., & Pearson, C. M. (2005). On the nature, consequences and remedies of workplace incivility: No time for "nice"? Think again. *Academy of Management Executive*, *19*(1), 7–18.

Porath, C., & Pearson, C. M. (2013). The price of incivility: Lack of respect hurts morale—and the bottom line. *Harvard Business Review*, *91*(1/2), 114–121.

Rose, K., Shuck, B., Twyford, D., & Bergman, M. (2015). Skunked: An integrative review exploring the consequences of the dysfunctional leaders and implications for those employees who work for them. *Human Resource Development Review*, *14*(1), 64–90. Available from http://dx.doi.org/10.1177/1534484314552437.

Sutton, R. I. (2010). *The no asshole rule: Building a civilized workplace and surviving one that isn't*. New York, NY: Business Plus.

Tepper, B. J. (2000). Consequences of abusive supervision. *Academy of Management Journal*, *43*(2), 178–190.

Whicker, M. L. (1996). *Toxic leaders: When organizations go bad*. Westport, CT: Quorum Books.

CHAPTER 3

What to Do About Toxic Leadership?

3.1 WHAT TO DO ABOUT THE SITUATION AT YOUR LIBRARY?

Before any action is taken by librarians, acknowledgment needs to occur at various levels in a university's hierarchy. This reporting process is easier if the higher education institution has established protocols to follow. If protocols have not been set up, then the onus of proving what happened or is happening falls on the reporting librarians. Documented incidents become important when librarians are asked to provide evidence of the claimed events (Henley, 2003; Lipinski & Crothers, 2014; Lipman-Blumen, 2005b; Pelletier, 2012).

3.2 DOCUMENTING INCIDENTS OF TOXIC BEHAVIOR

In order to facilitate the reporting process, it is extremely important to keep a journal, either at home or in an encrypted file on a work computer. Preferably, the incident log should be stored to the cloud or on a personal USB. Some librarians reported keeping their journals on their mobile phones. Even discussing every incident with a family member or a trusted friend who can keep notes is helpful, and better than not having any information written down from which incidents can be recalled in greater detail when needed.

3.3 BUILDING A SUPPORT NETWORK

Making allies among peers is of the utmost importance, as in this way more than one person can serve as a witness for the other and can also document incidents only they have witnessed. Many librarians reported having survived their horrific ordeals because they had peers they could trust. In fact, new alliances and friendships arose because colleagues had to hold so much confidential information for each other. Librarians

Academic Libraries and Toxic Leadership.
DOI: http://dx.doi.org/10.1016/B978-0-08-100637-5.00003-0
27

working as a team were able to circumnavigate their leader to fulfill their work duties and keep the library afloat for their users. This worked especially well when the toxic leaders were more interested in personal gain or were looking out for their favorite librarians.

Future potential witnesses can and should become an important part of the support network. These witnesses will be especially needed when reports come up for investigations, or when grievances eventually come up for review. Besides having documentation of myriads of incidents, librarians should also ask themselves if there are other witnesses they have neglected to include in their support network. It is best to be as well prepared as possible for this process. The high turnover that tends to occur in academic libraries with toxic leaders cannot be controlled by the remaining librarians. Witnesses may choose to back out if they believe that declaring what they saw could damage their livelihood. For whatever reason, witnesses may choose not to report what they saw, and that decision needs to be respected. This should not be seen as a setback; but instead whenever possible there should be more than one witness to call on. Maintaining ongoing relationships with witnesses is especially important when they have moved on to other jobs. Establishing a relationship in cases of toxic leadership is important, because once librarians have moved on to other jobs, in many instances they no longer wish to relive their negative work experiences.

3.3.1 Expanding the Support Network

When the toxic leader is first focused on someone, that person, most of the time, cannot believe it. They feel as if this could not really be happening to them. It has been described as surreal, topsy-turvy, transcendental even, but not in a good way. They have all wondered if others see it as well. Most librarians waited months or years before approaching others on the topic of the toxic leader, or toxic peers who were protected by the leader. These protégés are often spies for the toxic leader, when the leader is hands-on. Some toxic leaders, though, are more negligent or laissez-faire in their leadership style and simply let their favorites run wild within the library.

It takes time before the targeted librarian feels comfortable talking to other librarians. Many choose to keep what is happening to them to themselves, whereas other librarians seek support from a spouse, a friend, or a group of friends outside of the library. In many instances, librarians have realized it is not only them, but others as well, who are recipients of their toxic supervisors' special treatment. Although conditions do not necessarily change, just knowing that others know what is happening to them provides a sense of mental relief. The galvanization of librarians set against their toxic leader has helped many librarians survive without major negative consequences to their well-being or their jobs.

> We used to meet monthly then it changed to once a week. We were doing "Happy Hour therapy". We had to talk outside of work to cope and give each other tips. No one in upper administration was doing much about it. HR wasn't very helpful. We got real lucky, we had a good hire and the new director is good so far, things are changing.

Aside from leaving the institution, the truly final recourse is legal action. Well before legal action is even considered, librarians should attempt to gain allies in the higher echelons of the university's administration, if human resources personnel have proven themselves uncooperative or useless. Once all protocols have been exhausted, librarians may be left with legal action as their final choice, if the institution's administration is unwilling to remedy the library's toxic leadership situation. Always hoping to avoid a lawsuit, most institutions of higher education will seek mediation, an out-of-court settlement that possibly includes a gagging order for everyone involved.

3.3.2 Other Options

Throughout the period of abuse, sometimes the only option librarians have is to talk to someone trusted outside the library. The most reported option was talking with a psychologist outside of the institution. Ones who specialized in organizational culture and workplace insidiousness, if not toxic leadership itself, were the most sought-after for therapy treatments. These psychologists' expertise enabled librarians to cope with their new academic-library reality. Whilst some librarians sought psychological treatment through their employers' health insurance, others paid for private sessions themselves out of fear of having anyone find out they were seeking help to survive their toxic leader or peers.

Who else should academic librarians confide in besides family and friends? Religious leaders and spiritual guides were also reported as options deemed helpful by some librarians. Viable options became anyone who made librarians feel safe and offered a gathering space where they could speak freely about what was happening in their libraries without fear of repercussions.

3.4 WHO TO TALK TO ABOUT WHAT IS HAPPENING?

Academic librarians need to be sure they have thoroughly documented all incidents involving them or others. Regardless of how long it takes librarians to realize what is happening in their library as a whole or in a specific department, librarians need to document and report what is occurring there. Incidents can be reported to other supervisors within the library if they are deemed trustworthy. Union representatives may also be an option, and if that option exists it should definitely be explored. Human resources departments (whether or not they have employee protection protocols to handle whistle-blower incidents), or upper administration, for instance, a Vice-President of Academic Affairs, or a Provost, should be made aware of the situation in the campus library (Henley, 2003; Lipman-Blumen, 2005a, 2005b). Librarians may also wish to reach out to the Ombudsperson Office, if such a resource is available. In some cases, librarians had to contact the Vice-President or Provost of their institution directly because they had learned that their complaints were not being taken seriously by the human resources department.

Librarians may need to speak with colleagues in upper administration to find out if they will help, and not be left to wonder whether they condone the toxic leaders' behavior. For librarians who hold faculty status, reaching out to upper administrators such as the Vice-President, or Vice-Chancellor of Academic Affairs, could be the only choice if they want the library's toxic leadership situation to be handled and eventually resolved. At some institutions, Vice-Presidents became part of the librarians' support network and advocated for change in their libraries. At other times, librarians were either ignored by the Vice-President and other senior administrators or asked to figure it out themselves. In one specific case, figuring it out was the best advice. A team of librarians at a small institution explored a variety of strategies to remove their toxic leader. The planning took over a year, but once the plan was implemented the librarians successfully ousted their tormentor and were able to finally move their library forward.

Nevertheless, before an incident is reported, what librarians are sure they are experiencing or witnessing happening to peers (including support staff) needs to be documented. Without evidence to support claims librarians will not be taken seriously. Academic institutions have vast bureaucracies in most instances and as such they need to have substantial credible evidence before taking any action. Upper administrators need to know this is not a personal vendetta, hence their need to be circumspect regarding what may be considered an inconsequential accusation or a "he said, she said" situation.

3.5 THE CONSEQUENCES OF INACTION

The consequences of inaction for academic libraries can range from a negative impact on productivity to loss of reputation in and outside the higher education institution. These issues can improve with a change in the library's leadership, genuine support from the institution's upper administration, and time. It is only when the librarys' situation is taken seriously that bad situations such as demoralized librarians, loss of productivity, continuous turnover, and undermined user services can be improved. Yet this can only happen when action is taken. If no action is taken, then libraries can flounder for years, decades even. Lamentably, this has been the experience of some academic librarians. They witnessed their libraries slowly falling apart without anyone in power attempting to save or improve the library. Sometimes, it took scandals, high personnel turnover, having the local news channel or newspaper involved in reporting suspicious library operations and unscrupulous reorganizations of reference and instruction departments, before those in the institutions' administrations began a close examination of all that was happening in their libraries. Once the library received this much-needed attention, everything that had been happening in the library, and to its librarians, for years finally came to light.

The consequences of inaction for academic librarians are also many, though they are of a more personal nature. The ramifications of not acting in time or not wanting to recognize what is going on can be very damaging. It can lead to emotional problems, cause mild to severe health issues, and in extreme cases it accelerated death, as it was unfortunately reported by two librarians, who had the misfortune of witnessing the early demise of their fellow librarians.

The research for this book revealed many difficult conversations with academic librarians. There were librarians who reported they had sustained extreme stress and abuse for more than ten years and suffered from heart attacks (no family history of heart disease) or developed cancer where none had previously existed in their families. After years of working with a toxic leader, despite maintaining a healthy lifestyle, they had developed serious health problems all of a sudden.

Other librarians also had to handle burgeoning health problems ranging from migraines, insomnia, or exacerbated digestive syndromes to weight fluctuations. Weight issues came about either through stress eating or because of depression, anxiety, or conflict arising from the sense that they must show up to get their jobs done, but not draw any attention to themselves, made them drop their exercise routines. Others developed or increased unhealthy habits such as imbibing alcohol, smoking cigarettes, binge eating, or abusing sleeping pills. In one case, a librarian turned to hyper-athleticism in order to cope with the toxic stress at work. It was not surprising to learn that some librarians had also turned to legal and illegal drugs to escape the stress of being overworked and abused for years.

Many librarians admitted they had sought psychological help for feelings of inadequacy in their library and to cope with feelings of dissatisfaction because their toxic leaders did not care if they destroyed the library, they only cared about their own needs. There were also some librarians who said they went back to their church seeking spiritual guidance to withstand toxic leadership situations.

Feeling demoralized and not valued were the experiences most consistently reported by librarians, and which led many of them into a mild depression. There was also a small number of librarians, seven (out of the 54 interviewed), who suffered from Post-Traumatic Stress Disorder (PTSD). It was because they sought psychological help that they were in fact diagnosed with PTSD. They attended biweekly sessions (some were down to monthly when interviewed) to cope with their toxic environments. There were also two librarians who suspected they had PTSD and wanted to get a better handle on their work situation, but had not been able to find time to pursue their mental health because of work and family obligations.

Of the librarians who were diagnosed with depression, most sought treatment. A few librarians reported being diagnosed with clinical depression and were actively trying to get better and not have this affect their personal lives. Not having recourse to improve the toxic situation in the academic library can lead to extreme survival action to protect mental or physical health or both (Pelletier, 2012). Three librarians were very open about their struggles with horribly toxic leaders in their libraries. These librarians actually checked themselves into hospital. They were desperate for understanding and longed for things to make sense again. They knew they had exhausted the resources available to them via human resources or the librarians' union. In order to save their sanity, their last option in each case was to hospitalize themselves so as to have a much needed mental break. This time away from work gave them a chance to evaluate whether they wanted to return to their libraries. Incredibly, all three librarians returned to their jobs after this self-imposed leave. One of these cases was significantly more difficult than the other two, because, soon after being hospitalized, this particular librarian suffered a psychotic break. She was in care for 8 weeks and shortly afterward returned to work under a new library director. She was happy to report in her interview that she was thriving and getting along with her colleagues, and specially the new library director. The other two librarians' hospitalizations were for nervous breakdowns, and their stays were for 1 and 2 weeks. One librarian was transferred to another department and continues to struggle with micro-aggressions from her new supervisor, but the situation is tolerable when compared to her toxic leadership experience. The other librarian, regrettably, has not experienced much change, though she has adapted her outlook in order to handle the still unfair workload and excessive supervisory responsibilities. The fact that her Library Director is well regarded as a master of academic library workflow redesign only sustains the frustration. These trendy redesigns are typically damaging to morale and productivity. This librarian however keeps working toward achieving a better work-life balance.

In two cases, the consequences of inaction by two toxic leaders contributed to the decline in the overall health of their targeted librarians, which led to their eventual deaths on the job. According to the librarians who witnessed these events, their colleagues were consistently overworked, belittled publicly, either ignored or shouted at in meetings, and spurned for many years. Thus, even though these librarians may have had health problems to begin with, what contributed to their deteriorating health and ultimate demise was years of continual extremely stressful working conditions. These librarians believed they needed to go into work with a combative attitude in order to make it through the day. One of the witnesses, fearing becoming the next target, actively sought a position at another academic library. The other remained at her library because she had begun to document her Library Dean's toxic leadership. These cases are rare, fortunately.

At one academic library, at least five librarians from the same department, Technical Services, presented individual doctors' notes instructing whomever was in charge of the library to have them separated from the toxic leader. With their medical prescriptions, these librarians finally brought attention to their plight. They were separated from their toxic supervisor and an investigation into that department's leadership style was finally conducted. These librarians no longer suffered their toxic leader's abuse in silence. This clever solution achieved the removal of the toxic leader from their department, though it is disappointing to learn these librarians' previous complaints had been ignored by the Library Dean.

3.6 WHY STAY?

I can't go anywhere else really. My family is all here, in the area. Withstanding my boss would be harder if I did not have them near me.

Some readers may ask why these librarians did not leave that library, either by taking another job or by retiring from the profession. This is not as easy as it may seem, particularly if toxic leadership has not been part of their academic libraries' work experience. Through the interviews, librarians revealed a variety of reasons for staying in their positions. They were bound geographically owing to family obligations, or the job market in their desired area was nonexistent. Hence, without realistic employment alternatives these librarians had to remain and endure their toxic leaders. Other librarians felt strongly about not permitting a toxic boss to push them out of the jobs they enjoy and see as their lifetime career.

Where to go? Already middle aged, would have to start again so staying is the only option.

It should be noted, however, that in some instances leaving is the only solution. For these librarians' sake leaving is in their own best interests, but it must be thought out because, as some librarians sadly reported, they had either left for whatever job they were first offered or accepted a position that sounded better, only to end up in situations that were much worse than before. This is primarily due to the lack of transparency in the world of academic libraries. No one likes to talk about their toxic leaders, and thus academic libraries themselves, albeit inadvertently, continue to enable toxic leaders to take their leadership style from one library to another without major repercussions on their reputations. Some librarians observed that they had been in the profession for 15, 25, and over 32 years, and that they had never had a good, positive leader. They knew these terrible leaders were well regarded in the upper administrative world of academic libraries. These librarians wanted to start a dialog, because it needs to be happening if toxic leadership is to be reduced in academic libraries. In the end, it does not matter if librarians leave for another higher education institution, for that may not be the end of their toxic leadership experiences in academic libraries.

3.7 WHO BENEFITS FROM INACTION?

If you were one of his cronies you were treated quite well, you basically could come and go as you pleased, you could not do your job particularly well and you'd still get very high recommendations and good raises.

Regardless of how critical the situation in the academic library becomes, there are always those who benefit from the ensuing chaos. Those in the library who are treated well by toxic leaders, enjoy the consequences and wish the status quo to persist for as long as possible. These librarians typically do little work and are given the largest raises. Some are even engaged in peer-to-peer aggression, but they most surely praise and admire their leader and broadcast to the campus community that all is well in the library. Interviews revealed that in order to "show their humanity," most toxic leaders have a few favorite librarians whom they treat splendidly. Having favorites demonstrates to the campus community that they do care for their subordinates, or at least, treat them well. This, in turn, makes these preferred librarians speak very well of their leaders, because to them their leaders are not toxic. Such a farce can continue for years, even when it is obvious to everyone in the library who is being abused that quality and quantity of services have in many instances exponentially decreased, despite impotent librarians who keep giving 100% to their duties. These favorite librarians will continue to benefit as long as the toxic leaders remain in charge without any remedy in sight.

3.8 SUMMARY

The consequences of inaction affect librarians and library services, which in part affect users and the university community as a whole. The reason the academic library exists in the first place is to serve the campus community. Toxic leadership seems to be sensed once abusive behaviors are fully manifested in the academic library. Toxic leadership permeates the library environment, no matter what the size of the academic library. If the library is fortunate it could be that only one level within a hierarchy is affected. However, toxic leadership is known to infiltrate all levels, until the library and virtually all of the library's employees are negatively impacted (Lipman-Blumen, 2005a; Pelletier, 2012). For this reason, documenting, seeking allies outside of the library, and speaking about toxic leadership outside of the institution are important to make cases against toxic leadership more attainable (Henley, 2003; Lipman-Blumen, 2005b). The librarians interviewed for this book found these actions necessary if ending toxic leadership in their libraries was the desired outcome.

REFERENCES

Henley, K. (2003). Detoxifying a toxic leader. *Innovative Leader, 12*(6). Retrieved from <http://www.winstonbrill.com/bril001/html/article_index/articles/551-600/article578_body.html>.

Lipinski, J., & Crothers, L. M. (2014). *Bullying in the workplace: Causes, symptoms, and remedies*. New York, NY: Routledge.

Lipman-Blumen, J. (2005a). The allure of toxic leaders: Why followers rarely escape their clutches. *Ivey Business Journal, 69*(3), 1−8.

Lipman-Blumen, J. (2005b). Toxic leadership: When grand illusions masquerade as noble visions. *Leader to Leader, 2005*(36), 29−36. Available from http://dx.doi.org/10.1002/ltl.125.

Pelletier, K. L. (2012). Perceptions of and reactions to leader toxicity: Do leader-follower relationships and identification with victim matter?. *Leadership Quarterly, 23*, 412−424.

CHAPTER 4

Regaining Control of the Library

4.1 THE TOXIC LEADER HAS BEEN REMOVED, NOW WHAT?

The first step in regaining control of the academic library or department (in some instances) that has been under a toxic leader is to acknowledge what has happened. Attempts to minimize or dismiss the events are a disservice and belittle the suffering and damage librarians have endured. Regaining control of the library is a difficult task that must be undertaken because the toxic leader who is no longer there has in most cases left its librarians and staff in a demoralized state.

Once the toxic leaders have been removed or at least relegated to an area where they cannot continue to do the type of harm they have already caused it is time for the remaining library administration to establish rules, guidelines, protocols, and trainings dealing with this type of leader in order to prevent toxic leadership from recurring. If any of these steps are missed the likelihood of recurrence increases as proven by the experiences of librarians who have been in the profession for 15, 25, and more than 32 years and who have never had a good leader owing to toxic leadership and a lack of employee protection policies. Librarians who have suffered under a toxic leader must expose what happened and explain what ended up working in regard to coping and ending the abuse. These actions may include going to Human Resources to file a complaint, or to the Vice-President of Academic Affairs, the President, the union representative if applicable, or even the police (on or off campus) if threats of physical violence appear to be in the realm of possibility.

Regarding the selection of interim leadership, this library leader must be chosen carefully. This person, regardless of gender, needs to be compassionate and understanding of what has happened in the library. In over half of the interviews librarians revealed that their interim leader was usually a fellow survivor. Some of the interviewed librarians were the chosen interim directors and candidly expressed how they had learned how not to lead a library and that becoming the interim leader had inspired them to become department heads or library directors in order to model positive leadership. After what they had had to live through they wanted to

Academic Libraries and Toxic Leadership.
DOI: http://dx.doi.org/10.1016/B978-0-08-100637-5.00004-2

make sure that under their leadership librarians would not be abused and that the focus would be on making a better library for all departments through open communication and interdepartmental committee work. The word "transparency" was not used because in these librarians' experience library leaders who claimed to be transparent ultimately were not.

Once the new library leader has been selected, if the incoming leader is new to the academic institution, he/she needs need to be made fully aware of the situation by the Provost or someone else in higher administration. If this conversation is avoided or simply does not occur leaders may be caught off guard when subordinates start asking how long they will be there or ask what they think or have heard about what happened in the library. For this reason, procedures need to be set up to protect not only librarians, but also the academic institution.

4.2 MECHANISMS TO COUNTER TOXIC LEADERSHIP

The literature on toxic leadership indicates that it is important for an organization to have mechanisms for employees who want to report or challenge a toxic leader without feeling exposed and vulnerable (Lipman–Blumen, 2005b; Pelletier, 2012). Lipman–Blumen (2005a, 2005b) and Henley (2003) suggest the implementation of procedures such as contingency plans to help those who report abuse. Surprising as it may be, some organizations do not have whistle-blower policies or an office of "ombuds services," thus potentially leaving victims of toxic leadership feeling that they do not have much recourse at their institutions owing to the lack of established procedures to report what is happening to them (Kaminski & Sincox, 2012). Pelletier (2012) recommends that if these mechanisms are not already in place, then the organization should strive to be prepared for when the need to put these mechanisms into action arises, and all efforts should also be made to prevent the hiring of toxic leaders.

Within the academic library there should be policy development; it should not be left to the Human Resources Department, though they will need to play an integral part in this process. Together the academic library and Human Resources can generate policies that encourage a culture of communication, to openly speak without the fear of reprisals, policies that specifically spell out what behaviors are not tolerated. This should be taken as an opportunity to enumerate toxic behaviors and everyone involved should proceed in an efficient manner.

The ultimate goal is to stop the work environment from ever again becoming toxic. Academic libraries may have a slower transitioning of the complete staff (longer still if librarians are faculty), as is typical in academia, but eventually even institutional memory will not be enough, which is why it is imperative that mechanisms are enacted to prevent toxic leaders from entrenching themselves into the library again.

4.3 THE NEED FOR ACADEMIC LIBRARIES TO PRACTICE SELF-EXAMINATION

The librarian interviews revealed how some toxic leaders tend to move around from one academic library to another every few years. That the academic library culture needs to change was a view expressed hopefully by interviewees who know full well that the academic library profession is slow to change when it comes to people management.

There is a glass ceiling at the middle management level in academic libraries. Very traditional leadership is still going strong and library leaders do not want to hear about change.

When references are requested for a potential hire there is nothing wrong with saying that working with this person was difficult, but one should not exaggerate or cover up for a toxic leader by calling them a high impact leader or a strong leader. If one must use the term "high impact," then it needs to be qualified by saying if the impact was negative or positive. Academic library administrators are part of the problem if the accepted practice of covering up for toxic leaders continues simply because it has always been that way. This is a disservice to positive leaders, because the hiring process is rendered trivial.

Academic library administrators have to stop being complicit with the propagation of toxic leadership in the field. Whereas the majority of academic libraries are led by decent people, there is a significant number that are not. This fact came up frequently and it did not matter whether the institution was public or private, rural or urban, religiously affiliated or not, prestigious or not. In their interviews librarians declared their confusion about how toxic leaders were treated once caught beyond a doubt. It was difficult to comprehend how, if these toxic leaders were not retiring, they easily found another leadership position in another institution because the Vice-President or President had given them a good reference.

These toxic leaders were now another academic institution's problem. Academic library administrators have actively helped with the recycling and spread of toxic leadership because they have not been frank about their own experiences with toxic leaders. Instead of providing honest references they consciously chose to recommend, in effect passing on, the toxic leaders to the next unsuspecting library.

4.4 PROFESSIONAL LIBRARY ASSOCIATIONS LACK "PEOPLE TRAINING"

Disappointment was expressed by most of the mid-career academic librarians interviewed whenever professional library associations were discussed. These associations are perceived as just not doing enough, but charge what many librarians considered to be substantial fees for membership, to attend their conferences, and to participate in pre- or post-conference special workshops (at extra cost). Many librarians felt their associations should step up and play a stronger role in creating better training for mid-career librarians. Confidentially, they dared to speak up and stated that mentoring efforts need to extend beyond newly minted librarians or refined mentoring for already well-established library leaders. Mid-career librarians felt their associations' efforts toward their mentoring and leadership needs were virtually nonexistent. Academic library associations need to be more prominent when the issues around and ramifications of toxic leadership are discussed.

> I encountered real resistance to any guidance/mentoring, in fact it could be considered a closed door. They did not really want to deal with it, they wanted it to go away. I believe that as a library leader in higher education, the higher your aspirations, the more help you should seek, and my experience was that the higher I went, the less the help I found.

Of those interviewed, two library directors, acknowledged that the emphasis on "happy talk" in the library management literature needs to cease because it is damaging to the profession, for both new and mid-career librarians. These articles do not present the effort it takes to lead and maintain a successful academic library.

Library associations are missing an enormous opportunity to train librarians better to step into leadership and management, because it is known that these much-needed trainings are not happening in library schools. For example, the interview process (how to do a reference check what questions to ask when checking references, how to select for fit) and how to report a toxic leader or an abusive peer, among other topics could easily be given time every other year at associations' conferences. If these trainings and workshops are already happening for mid career librarians, then marketing and outreach efforts are not reaching those who need further education or are interested in exploring management and leadership positions in academic libraries. Finally, it would be remiss not to disclose that these trainings and workshops are probably prohibitively costly on a beginning or mid-career academic librarian's salary.

One can only imagine how much damage could be averted if librarians who come into management and leadership positions ill-prepared had the opportunity to participate in these professional development trainings. Certainly there would always be issues; people are people, that is not being denied. If academic librarians were better prepared many difficult work situations would be eliminated or at least conditions would be improved enough to prevent a situation from escalating to toxic leadership. Academic librarians need to be prepared to regain control of their work environment should the need ever arise.

4.5 MAINTAINING A NONTOXIC LEADER LIBRARY

It is important to maintain a toxic-leader-free library, because after the toxic leader has been removed (or isolated) the situation will not change for the better on its own. After the library has survived toxic leaders and their followers, it is time for the new library or renewed library leadership to take charge of the work needed to maintain a nontoxic-leader library. The easiest thing to do is not hire more toxic leaders, though this is not easy to execute. There are people, librarians included, who are very talented at gaming the interview process, while other toxic leaders are very obvious in their personalities and should not be hired, especially after the checking of references that are suspiciously pristine.

4.5.1 The Interview Process: Making it More Inclusive

The interview process needs to be improved by the inclusion of more questions about organizational fit and not relying solely on references. If there are lukewarm or generic references, these should be seen as a sign and not ignored. Even really positive references should be further investigated whenever possible. Background checks are useful, but these will not necessarily reveal whether their current employers are trying to rid themselves of their toxic leaders. Mendacity and denials of rumors were reported as common by interviewees who witnessed this practice when serving on search committees, in general. Allegedly this was done to avoid any probable future litigation and helping the toxic librarian to move on. For these reasons the reference checking process needs to be more deliberate. Whenever possible, both librarians and higher ranking administrators serving on the search committee should check references, to prevent the inadvertent hiring of toxic leaders with dubious references. It does not help matters that at many academic institutions, when there are large search committees, these tend to delegate the task of checking references to the search firm. Some librarians said this was done for legal reasons, but how helpful is it to the library to have a search firm looking out to answer the library's needs, particularly if that firm was not informed that the librarians are in the midst of recuperating from years of toxic leadership? Librarians should not be left out of the reference checking process, they know libraries best and most importantly, they know what type of leader they need in order to reinvigorate their library.

The final candidates for academic library leadership positions usually go through a 2-day interview process. During this time, the candidates need to talk to the librarians on a range of topics. Librarians representing all of the library departments need to engage with the candidates. Librarians also need to evaluate their potential new library directors for more than the typical 45-minute to 1-hour allotted session. At least three librarians need to be on the search committee. Two is often the number used for the library; however, there are more than two departments in a library and thus the need for broader library representation, especially on large search committees that have been charged with finding the library's new leader. Search committees have been known to have as many as 30 members, though even if the committee is just a dozen people, three of them still need to be librarians. With three of them on the committee, librarians can support each other when presenting their views or asking questions, or merely preventing other members' special interests from diluting the search process.

4.5.2 Selecting Interim Leaders From Within the Library

When middle-management positions needed interim leadership the interviews exposed how librarians were often selected to become the interim or next department leader simply because they were good at their jobs and not because they particularly wanted to serve as leaders. Therefore, no matter how wonderfully talented one may be as a cataloger, or reference or access services librarian, these job specific skills do not mean that these librarians will be productive and positive leaders. Being good at their jobs does not prepare these librarians to become good department heads or library leaders. Actual leadership potential must not be overlooked because unprepared or unwilling leaders do not create a positive working atmosphere. Many toxic leaders began their trajectory into leadership when they were forced into these positions, or saw a leadership position as their only opportunity for career advancement. Without proper leadership development or mentoring, some of these librarians eventually devolved into micromanagers who stifled innovation, or absent leaders with unreasonable productivity expectations.

4.6 THE ROLE HUMAN RESOURCES SHOULD BE PLAYING

Very large academic libraries operate their own Human Resources Departments, known as Library Human Resources. In small to medium libraries librarians do not have the option of having their own human resources department. These libraries must rely on the campus-wide human resources department. Unfortunately, relying on a generic human resources department is not very helpful to librarians because most human resources personnel do not understand the work that happens in the academic library, much less its role and function within the academic institution. To them librarians and library assistants who can be assigned ranks or levels are all the same. Human resources personnel struggle to differentiate between library and clerical positions, through no fault of their own. Advocacy from library leaders is much needed and this becomes evident when collaborating on policy creation or reclassifying evolving library positions. It is extremely important for human resources departments to recognize that librarians (whether they have faculty status or not) are valuable campus community members. The library leader should make this clear through advocacy and maintain the proper classification of new positions as academic libraries continue to develop and change to meet the emerging research needs of users. Only through advocacy will Human Resources stop their bias against the academic library as an innocuous unit on campus.

According to organizational psychology researchers there is not much research into how to deal with actual abusers in the workplace, regarding employee protection policies (Hurlic & Young, 2014; Loh, 2014).

Moreover, Loh (2014) states that the people "who are bullied tend to possess negative personality traits such as lack of self-control, lack of self-esteem, lack of self-confidence, poor social and communication skills" (p. 258–259). Fortunately, points of view like this one about victims of toxic leadership were not corroborated by the 54 academic librarian interviews compiled for this book. Many, if not most, of the academic librarians who were interviewed and reported having experienced toxic leadership, were and still are outgoing, confident, and excellent communicators who are passionate about their work. This is where organizational culture comes into play and where Human Resources can do more than be a bystander. It should not be forgotten that librarians are highly educated and their working conditions regarding toxic leadership or any consequences of negative leadership have not been studied before. The interviews also revealed that if there was rot at the top (in the highest leadership positions) of their academic institutions, the toxicity permeated all of the units, including the academic library. Needless to say, in these cases there is a much larger problem. Toxic leadership in academia, however, is not within the scope of this book. If toxic leadership in the academic library is to be seriously combated in the long term, then at a minimum the Vice-President of Academic Affairs, the new library leadership team, and Human Resources need to participate in the effort to create a positive work environment for everyone.

The Director of Human Resources or trained personnel can collaborate with the library's administration unit in the creation of policies that delineate toxic leadership behaviors and how these are not to be tolerated in the workplace. Human Resources should also have personnel trained to handle incidences of toxic leadership. These experts would suggest viable options to librarians who are dealing with a toxic leader, or who may want a confidential counseling referral. The policies created by these collaborations would include explicit directions on complaint handling, detailed investigation procedures, a clearly articulated resolution process, and also simple grievance procedures, which are already standard at many institutions of higher education. All of the academic institutions' employees who manage people will have to be trained and required to take leadership training to enable them to better communicate with, listen to, and get along with their peers and subordinates (Kusy & Holloway, 2009; Loh, 2014), as is already done with regard to sexual harassment or active shooter trainings.

A proactive human resources department should perform random audits all over campus, including the academic library. They should also send out confidential surveys, or outsource this function to ensure anonymity, if they are not already collecting data via online surveys (Loh, 2014). Trusting the integrity of the human resources department is important. It is problematic, however, as several interviews revealed, when the toxic leader is a good friend of the Human Resources Director or when the Director heeds only what the Vice-President for Academic Affairs deems appropriate. This is why mechanisms, which embolden librarians to contact administrators higher in the chain of command without fear of reprisals, need to be in place.

4.7 THE ROLE OF THE ACADEMIC INSTITUTION'S UPPER ADMINISTRATION

First, if a toxic leader is terminated the administration needs to refuse to provide future positive references and generous salary and compensation packages. An academic library is part of a larger institution and neither one should be acting as if they were a profit-making business, with extravagant severance and retirement packages. Academic institutions need to remember their mission, they exist to educate and to create new knowledge, not to monetarily enrich themselves and their fellow upper administration colleagues. This point of view was frankly stated by librarians who felt that there is too much coddling in academia's upper administration.

> That's the one thing we don't learn well as librarians, we're not in the higher education market for the money. I don't know about others, it makes you wonder.

Secondly, when hiring a library leader, the President and Vice-President need to recognize that they also are a part of the hiring process. The academic library is a very visible unit in the institution. At least the Vice-President of Academic Affairs, if not the chair of the search committee, has to demand from the final candidates some examples of past successes and to divulge how unsuccessful events were handled (Kusy & Holloway, 2009). These self-declared anecdotes can be revealing and have been found to be helpful when choosing the next library leader, whether it is for a position as dean or department head.

4.8 SUMMARY

Regaining control of the academic library after surviving toxic leadership is not as easy as it seems. There are many parts moving simultaneously and when one side, the academic library, does not have adequate skills concerted efforts must be made for their input to be heard by the other side. Ultimately, regaining control of the library is an institutional team endeavor that requires active participation from the academic library leadership, including all of its supervising librarians. The library's administration team needs to enact the new policies and must coordinate future toxic leadership reporting efforts if it is to be successful in their remediation.

REFERENCES

Henley, K. (2003). Detoxifying a toxic leader. *Innovative Leader, 12*(6). Retrieved from <http://www.winstonbrill.com/bril001/html/article_index/articles/551 600/article578_body.html>.

Hurlic, D., & Young, A. M. (2014). Policies for workplaces. In J. Lipinski, & L. M. Crothers (Eds.), *Bullying in the workplace: Causes, symptoms, and remedies* (pp. 321–335). New York, NY: Routledge.

Kaminski, M & Sincox, A. K. (2012). *Workplace bullying in health care: Peer-to-peer bullying of nurses.* Retrieved from <http://ilera2012.wharton.upenn.edu/RefereedPapers/KaminskiMichelle.pdf>.

Kusy, M. E., & Holloway, E. L. (2009). *Toxic workplace!: Managing toxic personalities and their systems of power.* San Francisco, CA: Jossey-Bass.

Lipman-Blumen, J. (2005a). The allure of toxic leaders: Why followers rarely escape their clutches. *Ivey Business Journal, 69*(3), 1–8.

Lipman-Blumen, J. (2005b). Toxic leadership: When grand illusions masquerade as noble visions. *Leader to Leader, 2005*(36), 29–36. <http://dx.doi.org/10.1002/ltl.125>.

Loh, J. (2014). The role of human resources. In J. Lipinski, & L. M. Crothers (Eds.), *Bullying in the workplace: Causes, symptoms, and remedies* (pp. 255–269). New York, NY: Routledge.

Pelletier, K. L. (2012). Perceptions of and reactions to leader toxicity: Do leader-follower relationships and identification with victim matter?. *Leadership Quarterly, 23*, 412–424.

CHAPTER 5

Healing for the Organization Free of Toxic Leaders

5.1 HEALING THE ACADEMIC LIBRARY FREE OF TOXIC LEADERS

The healing process should not be understated. Openly talking about what happened is extremely important for the library and librarians. Only through unimpeded communication can the permissive culture, which facilitated the toxic leadership's expansion of power, be discouraged from starting up again. If the academic institution's human resources department has created employee protection mechanisms, then library leaders and librarians can confidently move on to the healing process because a solid support system of policies has been established. This process varies greatly from academic library to academic library, yet it is usually influenced by the culture at large in the academic institution. Some are very proactive, whereas others are very slow to create employee protection policies against toxic leadership or policies in general.

The library's reputation on campus can be salvaged with nonstop advocacy from the new library's leadership and all remaining librarians. Outreach efforts will reap benefits, such as library events focusing on all members of the campus community, along with targeted events for students, faculty, staff and administration. Letting users know the library is fulfilling its mission to serve the campus community is important and a way to gain new allies.

If the library's tainted reputation has expanded beyond the campus, then it is probable there will be more damage, not only to the library, and it will impact the academic institution. When the harm done to librarians reaches regional news the work of healing in these libraries takes much longer. Even after years had passed there were always community members, and even librarians, who asked any librarians they encountered from "such and such" institution if they would discreetly share what happened. Community members and librarians like these are not asking out of concern, this is not about sharing; this is merely gossip and it should be avoided whenever possible. If it cannot be avoided, at this point the truth needs to be told, to halt rumors. Ultimately, the local scandal will be forgotten.

Academic Libraries and Toxic Leadership.
DOI: http://dx.doi.org/10.1016/B978-0-08-100637-5.00005-4
47

To assist the healing a culture of communication needs to be created to avoid toxic leadership from entrenching itself in the library's culture again. Cultures driven by ambiguous values have been proven not to work. Alternatively, tangible and behaviorally specific values can create a culture of personal responsibility and accountability (Kusy & Holloway, 2009) for the library's leadership. Administratively, the healing process is important because the library as a whole is then seen as revitalized and worthy of regaining the trust of the affected librarians and the campus community. Even so it will take time for librarians who need to express concerns of any type to learn to trust the leadership. They need time to adjust to the new rules, to trust that they will indeed be taken seriously, and not be ignored or considered out of line when reporting incidents which may not be pleasant for the library's administration to acknowledge. Initially there may be struggle, but nevertheless, after the new policies and the cultures of open communication and of personal responsibility and accountability are normalized, things will start flowing efficiently and lead to healing for the library that strives to continue to be free of toxic leaders.

5.2 HEALING FOR ACADEMIC LIBRARIANS

Having the toxic leader removed does more for librarians' emotional well-being than learning that new policies will be adopted to prevent toxic leadership in the library. Physically removing the toxic leader was a palpable action, unlike the implementation of procedures and policies, which depends on too many people. Nevertheless, an enormous part of the healing process for librarians will be learning that their academic institution has set up mechanisms for reporting toxic leadership and other types of abuse. Incidents may be reported freely without fear of reprisals of any type. This is significant because librarians will need to talk about what has happened. By talking about what has happened, librarians are able to process the fact that they are not alone and that what has happened to them should not happen to anyone. Removing the inevitable culture of silence which was instituted by the toxic leader is important, as are trainings and candid conversations pursuing authentic change in the library's culture, for the healing process to take place.

> When our library had a leader retire and another go elsewhere, everyone was thrilled to see the back of them. It is a pitiful thing when departures of long-time "leaders" result in glee, and not just for the library staff but employees from other areas of the university.

Even though some librarians declared that their academic institutions did not support their requests for assistance in handling their mentally and emotionally taxing work situations, most librarians reported receiving the desired professional assistance of psychologists or career counselors without any problems. Treatment allowed librarians to channel their energy in a positive direction and to focus on small achievable career goals. Other librarians began taking up old and new hobbies (e.g. knitting, hiking, bicycling, dancing, and cosplay among others) to break destructive coping mechanisms employed to deal with working in a toxic leadership environment.

As already mentioned, trusting a new library leader can take time for some librarians. It will be much harder for some than others because it will depend on the type and amount of abuse suffered by the librarians. It is much easier to begin having a positive outlook if the toxic leader was around for less than two years than if the abuse was allowed to continue for more than five years. Some librarians, in their interviews, unequivocally stated that they had worked only for toxic leaders. Librarians who were approaching retirement no longer harbored the hope of working under a positive and effective leader. It is hoped these librarians will find peace not only from the toxic leadership abuse they endured, but also in coming to accept that their work mattered and was valued by their peers.

I've had numerous really toxic library supervisors at four different [academic] libraries. The library profession is a magnet for toxic people, especially unfit managers; the reasons for this are not clear.

5.3 MINIMIZING RESIDUAL TOXICITY IN THE ACADEMIC LIBRARY

Residual toxicity merits mentioning because it can become an ongoing problem for some librarians if the healing process is not undertaken. Residual toxicity has been described by Wike (2015) as the long-lasting effects of a toxic leader on a person or a group. An example of this in the academic library might be when librarians are not able to focus on their work or are having a difficult time learning to trust the new library leader. These librarians are likely suffering from residual toxicity, and they believe something is going to happen again, they just do not know when. Any activities (e.g., programs, events, etc.) undertaken by the new library leader are mistrusted and these librarians are just waiting for something to come apart, to snap. This behavior does not benefit the newly established library dynamic. Leaders, therefore, need to be aware of residual toxicity. They also need to make sure they maintain open lines of communication to prevent their goals and objectives from being misinterpreted and unintentionally disrupted.

Librarians experiencing residual toxicity will find reminders of the toxic leader in the actions of the new leader. For some librarians, taking the time to speak to the new library leader about their concerns suffices and they are able to retake control of their duties without fearing retaliation. Other librarians, however, will have more difficulty trusting library leaders again. These librarians can come to respect and trust the library's new leadership only if they are genuinely good leaders who care about the library, their librarians, and if they in fact fulfill the mission of the library by advocating for the necessary resources and upper administration support needed to maintain a successful library.

> We have burnout, we have low morale, and we don't trust any process anymore. But this new leader seems like the real thing. I'm only willing to go through one more reorg, there's been five in seven years . . .

5.4 HEALING FOR LIBRARIANS WHO HAVE LEFT

Even librarians who have left the toxic workplace for another academic librarian position will need to deal with emotional and psychological consequences at some point in their lives. It is only after dealing with what happened that these librarians can truly move on. Of course some of the librarians interviewed spoke about moving on too soon or denying everything to themselves in order to cope and focus on their new jobs. Denial, however, works for only so long. In order to begin the healing process, librarians need to address what has happened to them even if they feel that it can never be reconciled logically. The leader's toxicity has nothing to do with the librarians themselves or the library. These librarians were merely carrying out their duties, some were just fulfilling their authentic passion for librarianship. Librarians who have been hurt this way need to accept that it was not their fault, believing and understanding this enable a crucial step to healing.

> Even normal healthy [librarians] that didn't have trauma in their personal lives, they all ended up traumatized because it's not normal that supervisors treat you that way. There's no reason why it should even happen. It was like I was living in a schizophrenic's brain. I saw a psychiatrist, it really helped me.

The exit interview may be cathartic for some librarians, and as such it must not be omitted when leaving the toxic leadership library. All of the toxic behaviors experienced or witnessed have to be reported in order to establish an official record of what occurred during the time the librarian worked there. Unfortunately, as was reported in the librarian interviews, in most cases exit interviews did not do much to change the toxic leadership culture for the librarians who remained. Nonetheless, exit interviews are essential vehicles for bringing attention to toxic leadership in the library. Responsible or well-prepared institutions have mechanisms to follow, and these facilitate the reporting process. This is exemplified in the closed cases of toxic department heads. These toxic leaders were isolated almost immediately by upper administration and reassigned to positions where they no longer supervised anyone. When the actual library director was the problem, then procedures changed and they were offered sensitivity training or coaching sessions on how to work better with subordinates. In most cases, where a toxic library director opted to leave they did not leave embarrassed or empty-handed, but left instead with a generous severance or retirement package. This was not the case for department heads, however.

> The library director had barely passed her 5-year review, she was almost fired, but the provost was leaving before a replacement could be found. So, the library director negotiated a deal, a clause was added to her 5-year contract stating that if she was not renewed, she would receive an extra year to work on a special project. She was kicked out 2 years later and got her extra year.

Disturbingly, some librarians reported seeing their old toxic leaders reassigned to special projects by the institution's upper administration, when the toxic leaders were close to retirement age. Interviewed librarians revealed they could only wish similar accommodations and considerations were extended also to librarians who had suffered under toxic leaders. Few of the librarians who opted to leave reported being offered job counseling by the human resources department. Some librarians left because they could not wait around for the toxic leaders to be removed, as regrettably, it is known typically to take a long time (years even) before a remedy is earnestly pursued. Fortunately, all of these librarians were able to find positions in other academic institutions. A couple of librarians admitted to still struggling with their toxic leadership experiences, with occasional flashbacks, and during their interviews said that they would pursue a few counseling sessions, to see if it could help them to move on and let go of this experience. All of these librarians were happy that they no longer worked for a toxic leader.

5.5 SUMMARY

Healing the library is not the same as healing the librarians. These are separate but interrelated processes that need to occur. Preferably they will happen simultaneously, and if this is not possible, then one should happen right after the other. Beginning with the healing of the library is best, because librarians will only begin their healing process once they know that they no longer work under a heinous toxic leader. To minimize residual toxicity open lines of communication must be created by the new library leadership, empowering librarians to freely communicate their fears and expectations of the new library leader and their roles as librarians. If leaving is the only path to beginning healing, then these librarians should be encouraged to perform an exit interview. Many things can be learned from these exit interviews after librarians have left the institution. Exit interviews can uncover warnings, expose troubling patterns and subcultures, and even provide solutions to the toxic leadership problems experienced by these librarians.

REFERENCES

Kusy, M. E., & Holloway, E. L. (2009). *Toxic workplace!: Managing toxic personalities and their systems of power.* San Francisco, CA: Jossey-Bass.
Wike, N.A. (2015, March 5). *Fallout: The residual effects of toxic leadership.* Retrieved from <https://medium.com/the-smoking-gun/fallout-e920065b2475>.

CHAPTER 6

Cases

6.1 INTRODUCTION

Toxic leadership is present in all types of academic libraries and at all levels of administration whether they are community colleges or prestigious large research intensive universities. The four cases presented in this chapter illustrate a variety of manifestations of how toxic leadership was experienced and handled at a variety of colleges and universities. Knowing what has happened in academic libraries, where it is suspected a toxic leader has taken over, can help prevent toxic leadership from permeating all of the departments in their library. Anyone who has worked for a toxic leader will recognize these behaviors and their effects on the academic library. Working in a toxic leadership environment as seen in previous chapters is not healthy psychologically, emotionally, or physically.

After analyzing 54 interviews, patterns emerged regardless of the size of the institution. The following four cases illustrate the most common and appalling actions done in academic libraries under the control of a toxic leader. All cases were based on in-depth interviews from more than one perspective. Each case is comprised of a minimum of eight librarians recounting their toxic leadership experiences. Interviews were overlaid to compose a more complete story of the toxic library leader based on Polkinghorne's (1995) analysis of narratives. Some of the librarian experiences presented have a resolution; others are still living under the miasma of a toxic leader.

Academic Libraries and Toxic Leadership.
DOI: http://dx.doi.org/10.1016/B978-0-08-100637-5.00006-6

Case 1

A national search was undertaken to find the next University Librarian (UL) and unfortunately the upper administration chose two poor library representatives to serve on the University Librarian Search Committee. In their eagerness to find someone to come in as soon as possible, the librarians missed the toxic leadership signs exhibited during the interview: only happy experiences throughout her whole career were mentioned along with evasive answers to question about fundraising expertise. The last thing these librarians expected was to go from a mediocre leader, who was known to like things to work out on their own, to a completely narcissistic toxic leader. Within the first six months the toxic leadership was out in the open. It began with dismissals of both librarians and library assistants who did not meet the new UL's library vision (a vision to this day no librarian is yet privy to) and the narrowing of the few communication paths available to her.

The UL had stated in her interview that she was well versed in library politics and well connected in the field. She promised to clean up the library and set it on a successful trajectory. During her first 2 years, she would continuously profess in library meetings that she would advocate for the library and make urgently needed improvements including a much-needed increase to the library's budget. She also promised to be transparent, have an open-door policy, and would not play favorites. The UL stressed to everyone that it was of utmost importance to work together if the library was to improve after having been led so poorly for the past decade.

More prominent issues began to arise when standard meeting dates were set for every month for an entire semester. Inopportunely, the UL would change these dates as she saw fit for the sake of her schedule. Librarians became upset because the once-per-month meetings became once-a-semester meetings and appointments had to be made well in advance to meet with her. The UL would be upset when timely appointments were not scheduled, but it was nearly impossible because she booked so quickly or was out. Librarians could never mention that she was out too much. The one librarian who did bring this up was rebuked for doing so.

Basic communication was never truly open, and by year two it was mostly nonexistent. Additionally, opportunities to participate and opine without restrictions or fear of repercussions had also disappeared. This was one aspect of meetings that many librarians relished because open discussions paved the way for future projects and enabled librarians to work with each other. Although the library's collection grew and services were expanded during the first 2 years, the expansion then decreased as the UL began to dedicate even more time to her professional associations' endeavors thereby leaving the librarians to fend for themselves more often with each passing year.

During this time the UL's proclamations became more bombastic. Some librarians began to see her as power hungry and delusional because she was always citing her colleagues in the field as well as studies, but references to these studies were never provided. She had also become careless and let it be known who her favorite librarians were. These were primarily incompetent or inexperienced librarians who were nonthreatening to her. To everyone else who worked in the library it had become clear that her way was the best way to run a library.

She manages by intimidation she manages by trying to pinpoint the person's weakness and playing on that weakness. She has a chaotic style that I think really makes it difficult for the library to figure out what it is we're doing.

The UL would not listen to how things were done in the past. It infuriated her when librarians questioned her and she would show her disgust and verbally abused the librarians who spoke up in meetings. She enjoyed threatening librarians mostly in private though there were times when she would threaten the whole library staff all at once. She was vindictive and would ostracize librarians until she needed them again. It would be a semester or two before a librarian joined the rest of them in meetings. Although the library before this UL never had a culture of collegiality it had neither ever been truly competitive. It had been mostly a live and let live type of place while the abuse of a particular set of librarians was carried out discreetly. Under this UL there was visible animosity and discontent against some librarians.

[The UL] shoots from the hip all the time. She can be amazingly lax about certain things for certain people and then amazingly tough on others, there's a lack of fairness.

Under the UL's toxic leadership the library had become an obstacle course and only librarians who were in her inner circle would be assisted through the course. Expenses for professional development were a constant issue for disagreements. Her favorites could spend funds however they liked whereas no one else was afforded such liberty. The UL would "especially allow male librarians to get away with murder in all aspects of their duties." Her favorites received the largest raises at the end of year regardless of how hard they worked.

Her narcissistic tendencies also became more prominent when she presented herself as all seeing and all knowing. Librarians could not question her pronouncements even when they were clearly misinformed. She enjoyed giving monologues about her connections in the profession and how these made her who she was. Sadly, she was not as well connected as she fancied herself to be: after 4 years her fundraising team had received only a few pathetically small donations.

The UL overworked librarians who worked for the sake of the library's mission because they were necessary to keep the library functioning. If these librarians asked for anything be it resources, to establish new services, or raises, she would become irritated. Some librarians were told that they needed to make sacrifices for the overall health of the library, but this stricture never applied to her favorites nor to herself. Inevitably, resentment grew among the overworked librarians, which continues to help spread toxic leadership throughout the whole library. There were some librarians she used from time to time and others she completely ignored. The UL's lack of communication skills, combined with her often leaving for business or vacation without it being communicated to the librarians, created mistrust. The UL also created silos were none existed before. She hated being called out on mistakes or needed improvements. She would only listen to these when they came from her favorites.

There is always fear, a feeling of fear and there is a contamination. People aren't as friendly or as open because I believe there is a lot of stuff going on underneath the surface.

She would nit-pick ideas, research agendas, and professional desires of some librarians, and would push through terrible ideas simply because these came from one of her favorites. Some of these ideas cost the library a small fortune and were never executed again. And even though all librarians were told there would be an opportunity to provide feedback for all executed ideas, the feedback opportunity for one particularly costly and disastrous event was canceled and replaced with a library promotion and marketing exercise. All ideas, even bad ideas, would be considered provided they came from certain librarians.

It's so chaotic and it's really hard to figure out how to prioritize your own work because her chaotic style means that she has no regard for your own work and what she needs come first. Everything stops until she gets what she wants. It's exhausting.

The UL believed herself to be a people person and took pride in being able to hire competent librarians. Of her 6 hires after 4 years only 2 librarians remain. New hires did not receive positive reinforcement or proper training. Instead they were simply overworked from day one and asked to meet ridiculous expectations that were generally given at the last minute. The UL only wanted results and did not care how these happened. All the librarians were by now sharing among each other how the UL never clearly articulated what her plans were. The UL's pattern of bad hires is covered up in the interview process by her saying she gives new and mid-career librarians a chance to grow before moving to other positions.

Remarkably, this UL believes herself to be a wonderful mentor. She believes her mentoring method is productive even if she has to terrorize her mentees who never asked for her mentorship in the first place. She strongly pressures them to produce presentations and shames them when they do not.

She [UL] seems to misunderstand mentoring. She thinks it's just pushing and I think sometimes it's a push, but it's more than just pushing. She expects a lot and she burns people out. It's not healthy.

Her mentoring program has been counterproductive, as it has led most of the newer librarians to seek psychological assistance to cope with their extremely high stress and a variety of other symptoms ranging from insomnia, loss of morale, weight fluctuations, drinking, and walking around with a never-ending feeling of dread regarding what the UL will ask them to do next.

Throughout the years she has reduced her advocacy for the library and has not really demanded a larger budget to at least keep up with the basic inflationary needs for raises and collection growth. At first, like most toxic leaders, she promised a lot of things. After years of empty promises a pattern has been set. She no longer cares about creating a successful team of librarians, in retrospect she probably never did. Most of the library's personnel is demoralized, less productive, does not feel valued and is confused. The library is minimally meeting its goals but it is not growing. Due to toxic leadership and poor hires librarian turnover is now an inevitable common occurrence. Librarian searches have become ongoing. They cost a lot of time and money and have become a drain on the university's recruitment resources.

I don't believe the upper level people take this seriously. They're the ones that have the power to make a difference and they're not.

During the fourth year of her reign, there was a change in the university's upper administration. The UL would now have a new supervisor, the Vice-President of Academic Affairs (VP). This new VP was solely an interim and as such did not get much involved in the library. This was all the information the UL needed for her to go after librarians that were not meeting her expectations. She micromanaged those librarians she wanted out of her library. Most of the hardworking librarians have reached an impasse, they do not know where to go, they have been silent for so long. They do not trust the Vice-President because as an interim he is perceived as distant and weak. He does not like conflict. A few librarians have met with him in person and have written formal complaints against the UL still nothing has happened. Some librarians come up with excuses such as complaints against deans and directors take time because they need to reach a critical mass at this university to merit an investigation.

> I don't think this institution has stepped up to the plate to deal with everything. It's a level here that I just did not think was possible, beyond belief…nothing could have prepared me for this endemic system, it's institution wide. I mean it's just institutionally systemically toxic and I had never seen anything like this in all of the academic libraries I've worked.

This brash UL went in taking walls down only to then erect stronger and higher ones to suit her own needs. To function the librarians who care about the library circumvent the UL often and simply seek forgiveness for their successful events and procedure implementations after these have taken place. After the UL's anger has subsided she takes full credit for these events. When things do not go well she easily blames her librarians for issues triggered by her neglect. The constant withholding of information, scolding and disparaging of librarians in public, her narcissism, the persistent creation of silos, never being allowed to question her authority, spending lavishly on herself, secret meetings, spending more and more time away from the library to help other libraries improve, remaining active in professional associations to the detriment of her leadership and management of her own library, taking vacation whenever large projects were undertaken by the library make her a toxic leader. She does not like problems, she just wants all of the benefits without any of the work. The UL, albeit an older woman, has a lot of years ahead of her to destroy the library if she is not stopped soon. The damage has begun, and it is up to upper management to step in to remedy the situation seeing that they have had the facts for years.

DISCUSSION QUESTIONS

1. What should the librarians do to improve their circumstances?
2. Do you agree that is it time for this divisive UL to leave the institution?
3. What characteristics would describe the UL as a toxic leader?

Case 2

This library director (LD) was the second director ever at this university library. He seemed to be a fair leader at the beginning. He expanded user services and updated the library with much-needed technologies (e.g. state of the art ILS and establishing a web presence). He even advocated for a larger budget that would cover more than just annual inflationary needs. However, once he was comfortable in his new role as LD innovation began to slow down and creativity was strongly discouraged. He did not bother with requesting adequate funding for the library because the library was finally the way he wanted it to be. The LD would build his administrative team with like-minded librarians who would in time turn on their coworkers. These events after years of toxic leadership rendered "a really poorly functioning, a poorly funded, an underused, poorly housed library with a highly demoralized staff." Publicly he was known as a very nice man, but privately he would intimidate librarians, especially women, and could be extremely patronizing.

> His appearance of taking care of the library was more important than actually getting library work done. Where we are actually discouraged from doing anything. I think it comes from [LD's] insecurity.

This was the LD's third library directorship, and as he aged into what would be his last LD position he became more dependent on his associate university librarian (AUL) and his favorite librarians. The AUL, who was also one of the LD's favorites, would take advantage of the LD's protection and failing health to abuse her coworkers. After the initial 2 years of hard work with updating and expanding user services, the LD moved on to perfect his library. He began to fire difficult female personnel and replaced them with males. The various exit interviews given by the women who were forced out did not matter much because the LD had a great relationship with the human resources director. In less than 5 years, the library's hardworking culture (although never very innovative) transformed into a laissez-faire one and maintained the status quo.

What made this LD a toxic leader, according to the librarians who worked for him, was his tendency for favoritism, poor communication skills, and fear of innovation, starting with the 2.0 revolution in libraries. At the end of his career his aversion to making decisions became more of an issue. His solution to innovation was to ignore new trends. Favoritism was the most obvious flaw, and if the LD did not like someone in the library, he and his favorites would make it difficult for that person to work in the library. One of the librarians realized that "there was no leadership guidance. There was no guidance coming from neither the person who'd been assigned my mentor nor the actual LD in power."

Librarians who excelled in their jobs and were active in the profession were punished by the LD for making the others look bad and accused by the AUL of setting higher standards for everyone. Some of the librarians felt it was unfair that they had to show up to work every day to work while the favorites only needed to show up for at least an hour a day to get paid. The AUL routinely informed these librarians that they were not team players and they were punished by giving them negative review letters and were personally attacked at librarians' meetings. Moreover, depending on how upset the AUL had become she would pass on their projects to other librarians.

As time progressed the LD allowed himself to be influenced by his AUL to the point that some librarians' raises were in fact decided by the AUL. There were a couple of single female librarians who were denied their complete raises because as they were neither married nor had children they did not need a full raise even if they had earned it. By complete raise it was meant that those who had family obligations and did their job received for example 5% and those who had no one to be responsible for received 4.5% or less. It depended on what the AUL had decided and if the LD would dispute or accept it. Most of the time he accepted the raises and would inform librarians of the change in raise. For many years, raises were affected by the AUL's manipulations. She would decide if you had been good to her the previous year on a whim. The rationalizations given to librarians became more and more bizarre with each passing year. The affected librarians would later learn that this was a type of financial bullying that the LD fully participated in to favor his sycophants.

The toxic leadership style this LD exhibited was relentlessly passive-aggressive. He would make promises that he would later deny or only kept because there were witnesses to his initial promise. One salient promise was allowing a librarian to attend an all-expenses-paid conference outside of the country. When the librarian returned from said conference she submitted the appropriate expense reports and receipts as required. She was initially denied reimbursement because the LD could not remember meeting with this librarian much less promising her monetary funding to attend a conference so far away. Fortunately, his secretary witnessed the librarian leaving the LD's office in tears and asked what was going on. Upon realizing the misunderstanding the secretary checked her files and handed the LD the handwritten note he had given her months prior to the conference. This secretary was punished for her actions, but she informed the librarian to not worry about her as she knew how to handle her boss's anger.

Near the end of the LD's tenure the AUL began to control more of the daily responsibilities. Newly hired librarians were led to believe by the AUL that she would take care of them and be their go-to person and so they did not bother the LD with needless concerns. This so-called change of command (although not legitimate) allowed for the AUL and the LD's favorites to go after librarians who were not maintaining the status quo. The peer-on-peer abuse or bullying at this library was at first ignored because it was deemed invisible. The librarians experiencing the abuse could not believe what was happening to them. Initially it was two librarians who the favorites went after. It took the persecuted librarians a full year to realize that what was happening was happening to both of them. This was very fortuitous because in the experience of many librarians who were interviewed for this book it usually takes many years before librarians realize they are not the sole victims. These librarians teamed up and were able to watch out for each other.

Unfortunately, they were too few against the barrage of rumors about them and their professionalism that was spread all over campus. Each fall, when the librarians would return to work, they came back to expressions such as, "Oh, we thought you weren't coming back!" from their liaison faculty and even library staff. Initially the librarians would ask "Who told you that? Where did you hear that?" These questions were met with "Oh, never mind, glad to see you" or "Does it really matter?," which, of course, it did matter. Guarding their reputations became an all-consuming endeavor for these librarians. It was thoroughly exhausting because no matter how hard these librarians tried they could not keep up with the endless rumor mill. These assaults on their professionalism were exacerbated by the fact that the LD refused to believe his AUL and favorite librarians would behave in such an untoward manner. He actually accused the attacked librarians of fabricating these rumors and of bringing whatever happened to them upon themselves for not maintaining the status quo. He even asked them to put their brains on the back burner in order to maintain order in the library. These librarians were punished with small raises and given less funding for professional development activities. The LD really disliked problems, which is why he believed in having a laissez-faire environment in his library, a place where everyone had their place. Hence, innovation and creativity were only allowed in tiny amounts and only when it came from the AUL or one his favorite librarians.

> I was treated horribly. I was publishing, doing presentations, I was doing things, but I did not choose to be open with my supervisors and colleagues because I found that it did more harm ... It really became a hostile environment...Decisions were no longer being made for the good of the institution, the good of the students, the good of the faculty...it was really personal attachments and vendettas that were driving the decisions...you can't be productive when that's the case.

After 20 years of a permissive toxic leadership influenced culture it inescapably permeated the whole library. No department was left untouched. The toxicity was so rampant that many instructional services ceased and the Access Services Department had become a revolving door. They could not keep their personnel. The Instruction Department was so dysfunctional that it could only handle the basic library orientations. No one was willing to put in extra effort. For what? Those librarians would only be punished in the end for doing too much. Faculty had spoken up because the atmosphere in the library had changed drastically. Many no longer felt comfortable going in to do their research but it took years of complaints to bring awareness to what was going on.

> My HR complaint was really illuminating to me. It crushed me being so naïve to thinking that everybody else that worked in academia also had the same morals and ideals that I did ... I was very shocked that the people really high up in power were so dismissive and kind of didn't really care what was going on. I was not the first squeaky wheel that came out of the library...

It was this most obvious situation that eventually caught the attention of some in the university's upper administration. The toxic leaders had taken their abuse too far that finally the office of the Vice-President of Academic Affairs became involved. A librarian was publicly humiliated by an AUL's protégé. Librarians could not complain to "the Human Resources Department [because it] was next to ineffective and if anything, basically was only there to deal with the most minor issues staff would encounter." It was a librarian and a staff person issue that revealed the truth, and as a result there was an eight-month investigation, which uncovered a disturbing truth: the LD and his favorite librarians, along with his AUL, were acting like a mob. Their threats and constant lies enabled them to control all of the library's personnel and had led to the forcing out of female employees for at least a decade. The culture of silence made it difficult for the Vice-President of Academic Affairs to decipher what was really happening in the library. The LD could not ignore that there were issues (librarians drinking publicly, user services severely reduced, peer-on-peer personal attacks, etc.) in his library, and knowing that he was part of the problem and that he did not have the energy to remedy the situation, he decided to retire immediately.

In essence the LD was forced to step down because of his toxic leadership that not only he exercised but also because he exercised it with the AUL along with his favorites. The AUL took it upon herself to abuse and fire and hire as she pleased and kept the LD in the dark and when informed he only said the AUL was doing what was best for the library. For his troubles the forced-out LD received a very generous farewell compensation package that included salary for one more year and allowed him to do his work from home while a national search was carried out to find his replacement. Knowing that the LD would still be around when the new LD arrived made for awkward interactions between them even if this interaction only lasted 2 months. More careful planning should have taken place to avoid a possible clash between the old and the new library leadership.

DISCUSSION QUESTIONS

1. What could have the librarians have done to improve their circumstances?
2. Was forcing this LD into retirement ultimately the right thing to do?
3. What characteristics make the LD a toxic leader?

Case 3

A very well-respected academic library unfortunately was led by a truly toxic leader as stated by librarians who worked for her. For a moment, the situation in the library seemed to continue without remedy in sight. Before becoming the director of the library (DL) she was another highly educated and well-prepared librarian with vast experience in academia who was deemed a go-to team player. However, once the library's leadership fell into her hands she changed into a tyrannical egomaniac whose new job it seemed was to poison all librarians' trust in each other, to berate them publicly and privately, as well as engage in nonstop micromanaging.

After enduring years of toxic leadership, most if not all of the librarians complained to the university's Vice-President and the President at least once. Unfortunately, the college's upper administration refused to take sides, claiming that because all of the librarians involved in the toxic dynamic was among faculty and as such should be handled through dialogue and biennial leadership position elections. These librarians were mostly women and were considered a homogeneous group even though they clearly belonged to very distinct ethnic groups, religions, and social classes. Due to the perceived homogeneity in the library unit by upper administration there was no actual conflict requiring their involvement. This attitude is troubling because even if this group of librarians is considered homogenous, the power dynamic is not being taken into consideration and is purposefully being minimized. The power balance needed to be acknowledged, and because it was not the DL took advantage of the lack of interest from her supervisors, and continued to terrorize her librarians for years.

> Lashing out, picking on someone to hate, have witnesses so others learn not to make her angry, "She [DL] came into my office and took me by the arm to another office closed the door and screamed at him [male librarian] …I just stood there I was in shock I'd never seen her like that. She was out of control then she opened the door, [calmly] walked out, had me walk out [she closed the door and left]. I didn't know what to do…"

This DL, like many other directors, is middle aged, narcissistic, and has a mean streak. Her toxicity is now legendary for her love of power and for her dislike of being contradicted. She fancies herself an expert and mentor to her personally selected incoming librarians. She keeps an open relationship with the college's higher administration in order to maintain their support. The director does not push or challenge as much as she could to help the library's position on campus. She tries to keep her librarians and staff in check. She appreciates innovation as long as she is included in the efforts and given credit. A librarian stated, "I learned really fast...that a whole lot of ideas is not appreciated, within my library it's like be quiet." whereas another disclosed that her work on a major education initiative was stolen and used by the whole system of libraries without the DL fighting for recognition. The DL knew this issue was not worth the use of her political capital.

All of the librarians were overworked, constantly berated, intimidated, and abused in front of other librarians and library staff. Some were told repeatedly how they were worthless and blamed for not doing their jobs well, even when strained due to the cramped working conditions. The DL did not advocate for her librarians when they had to deal with a temporary relocation.

> Who suffers the most is the campus and students because this library's a shadow of what it could be. We could be doing so much for students and we are doing almost none of it. We don't have the space it's hurting the library's reputation on campus...a lot of people now find the library and the librarians ridiculous but our DL won't let us do our jobs.

The librarians who spent over 2 years in a cramped shared space expressed a range of symptoms due to working for a toxic leader. They have experienced high stress and health problems due to the harsh work environment they had to endure for longer than the originally stipulated 6 months. The symptoms ranged from feeling down, insomnia, psychological distress, and emotional issues regarding their job security. It did not help that everyone was aware of how much the DL enjoyed pitting librarians against each other at meetings. Librarians and library staff have overheard the DL more than once stating that "'Sometimes I just like to watch them [librarians] fight' and she either directly instigates or she lets the fighting continue instead of doing the more appropriate thing. From what I've lived through the fighting seems to reenergize her." The DL eventually revealed that she chose the one-room office solution during the temporary relocation to build a stronger team and make sure everyone was working their hours.

> I could not have ever thought of just some of the craziness that I honestly have experienced. I really had a naiveté about higher education that was completely blown out of the water of how these people behave they are highly educated... I did (eventually) realize it was not about me, but I also realized that there is a kind of Kool Aid to higher education that they all drink.

Not knowing when the next confrontation with the DL would be kept some of the librarians constantly stressed out and had some return back to their old bad habits such as smoking, eating junk food, abandoning special diets, and exercise regimens, among others. Sadly, a few of these librarians also began to exhibit classic Post Traumatic Stress Disorder (PTSD) symptoms such as loss of sleep due to recurring nightmares, severe anxiety, flashbacks, and constantly reliving passed traumatic episodes where they were belittled in public or forced to work under the DL's close supervision. Some librarians also showed effects on their personal lives with a constant fear of going in to work and needing to have family members drive them to work. Their health was also affected. Some of the effects were losing dental fillings and not being able to focus on the present as well as being diagnosed for varying degrees of depression.

You just live with it every day, like I just, I know it's there. And sometimes when something really bad happens I get really upset and then I can't stop. ... it takes me a while to calm down from it. But in general, it's become an old wound, it's just there with me all the time.

This college's upper administration chose to not step in and stop the toxic leadership by considering all of the librarians as equals even though the librarians knew their DL was a toxic leader who not only abused them, but also dedicated time to abusing the untenured librarians. At this college, the DL position can change every 2 years because librarians are all faculty with shared governance and the library is regarded as another campus academic department. If the librarians were to vote against her reelection, the DL openly threatened she would ensure they were not awarded tenure.

Most the librarians working in this library came from other system campuses and other parts of the country because they had heard how professional and respectful the college system in general was toward librarians. Here librarians were faculty and participated fully in the college's governance. Librarians had a hard time reconciling who they were, their work ethic, and their intolerable work conditions. The emotional abuse took its toll and affected their work in some instances. For some librarians, the constant berating and lack of confidence in their abilities by the DL fueled their work outside the library, while other librarians became demoralized and needed to seek therapy to help them cope with their hopeless situation.

It would take a little over 2 years to galvanize and unify most of the librarians against this extremely well-connected DL.

She's got friends in all the right places...The HR guy is her friend so I can't go to him, you can't go anywhere, there's nowhere to go. She doesn't have many friends but the ones she made are the right ones to have.

The unifying took time because librarians needed to know who they could really trust and who they assumed would run immediately to the DL and inform her of the librarians' plan to oust her from her DL position. Early on the librarians knew it would be impossible to recruit the DL's two sycophants thus they worked quietly to not give rise to any suspicions. They all still worked in one large room without any dividers for privacy. The demoralized librarians were no more. They finally had a plan to remedy their intolerable work environment. They knew their only chance to bringing change to their library was going to be by exercising their vote in a future election.

> What keeps me holding on is my dream, [it] has become that three or five years from now the library's is going to be so amazing that no one's going to believe that [DL] ran it for 15 years. That's my dream that people won't believe this library was not ever such a great place to work...that's what keeps me going.

The biggest decision the librarians had to make was who would be the librarian among them to run against the DL. After thinking it through the librarian chosen was someone strong, fair, and tired of the maltreatment. She was also secure in her abilities and well respected on campus. It was then time to execute their plan. The librarians knew that on the first day of voting the DL would remind them all to vote for her. This was in fact not a reminder, it was just another opportunity the DL took to intimidate all of the librarians. The librarians would only prevail if they voted as a block against the DL on the first day of voting, which they did and it worked. It had to be done that way as it was the only way the librarians could listen to the DL without being persuaded into voting for her, as the votes would have already been cast. The librarians were able to secure their liberation from their toxic leader, but what was not thought out was what would happen after taking down the DL. The librarians now needed to be mentally prepared for the consequences of the DL losing her power and position. How quickly could their new DL begin advocating for them to upper administration?

The librarians defeated their toxic leader with careful execution of the plan. There was finally new leadership in the library unit after fifteen years of toxic leadership. Change could finally happen, but how? How fast? Although taking down the old DL was necessary to improve the library, some librarians felt that they had not spent the necessary time building alliances with upper administration and that this would affect the new leadership in the library. The status quo had been maintained for so long that no one was expecting the librarians to take down their DL any time soon. Their ex-toxic leader was now a colleague who would share teaching responsibilities with them. The old DL would want to share her expertise with the new DL for leadership continuity purposes. The ex-toxic leader played the game because she was the only librarian who had established connections on campus. She was extremely angered by the vote and so resorted to being strategic in all of her actions. Every chance she gets she leverages her political capital. Although defeated, the ex-toxic leader is still a presence. The new DL has isolated her, yet she still tries to exercise her power and influence. Everyone in the library is hoping the ex-toxic leader will retire soon or at a minimum start phased retirement.

Defeating a toxic leader is possible. However, the planning must be strategic and done well in advanced as it was done by this team of academic librarians. If these steps are not taken it can lead to awkward situations that may impede a speedy trajectory toward healing the library because the buy-in needed from upper administration is not automatic. Strong support needs to be carefully cultivated. Regardless of the politics still at play the library is in a much better place. Librarians do no regret the risk they took as a team to build the library their users deserve. Yet taking over a severely damaged library is a lot hard work as the new DL discovered. The new DL was ultimately assisted by some in upper administration and was encouraged to take leadership institutes to help her with improving the library's morale and productivity. The new DL has had to work hard and as fast as she could to ensure positive changes take root and not consider the possibility of losing her, their new leader in the upcoming elections.

DISCUSSION QUESTIONS

1. What could have the librarians done to improve their circumstances?
2. Should the toxic leader be integrated into the librarian's work circle or moved to a special assignment to enable change in the library?
3. What characteristics make the DL a toxic leader?

Case 4

Ageism, delusions of grandeur, threats, misinformation, deceit, and belittling were this leader's most common methods to getting her way. The toxic leader in an academic library is not always the Library Dean. It can be a department chair (DC) or any other supervisor. At this university library, the dean, a woman known to rule with an iron hand, did everything in her power to enable a young and talented librarian in the hopes of having her become her successor. This DC would become a relentless tyrant to her peers and library support staff with the dean's blessing. The dean for years purposefully turned a blind eye to the toxic work environment being created by her favorite because these years were considered formative and mistakes were to be expected from this soon-to-be powerful emerging leader. The library dean herself was well known for a great moment of library leadership she had performed in the 1990s. She was still resting off those laurels. The dean believed herself to be a wonderful leader and mentor who liked to groom librarians in whom she saw leadership potential and a little of her own mean streak. According to librarians who worked for the dean, she was known to say that if a leader came across as too nice it would come across as weakness.

Once the dean appointed her as the new instruction DC, it would take a little over two academic years before this library department became a revolving door. The DC expected all new hires to do her personal research and prepare her conference presentations. Newly hired librarians at first felt compelled to do it because they did not feel they could say no to the DC. These librarians were promised coauthorship for their efforts, but this never happened for any of them. The DC only used new hires for her own benefit and never provided any direction regarding their duties or expectations before their next review. When asked for a meeting the DC was always busy or would cancel at the last minute.

> She was extremely self-centred and did not care about anyone or the library. She only cared about her own needs. I feared retaliation and didn't speak because I felt it would only hurt me in my next review.

Librarians in the Instruction Department were under high stress and in constant fear of not getting a good review.

> There was a lot of evidence of stress that I wasn't even aware that was taking place. It was affecting me physically and I began to get bald spots on my

scalp...I don't feel like I could do anymore because I was already stretched beyond my limits...

Things would remain the same for four more years. The Instruction Department had earned its bad reputation within the library, yet the dean did nothing because she considered the up and downs of a department to be normal. Eventually the DC would find her stride. After the library dean retired a year later everyone was happy to see her go because it was time for new blood to reenergize the library. The new library dean, a man, decided to hire a replacement for the newly vacant associate dean position because the previous associate dean had retired after helping the new dean transition into his position. The now considered, well-groomed and officially hated DC of the instruction department felt this was the time to make her move into upper administration. She strongly believed she was owed the associate dean position because the previous dean had personally informed her of her true leadership potential. Members of the Associate Dean Search Committee were confused because they did not receive any internal recommendations, the DC had recommended herself at the last minute. In order to learn more about the library, the new library dean opened up the opportunity for feedback in every library department to provide the DC a fair opportunity for the associate dean position. The dean had only worked with this DC for a year and he had seen how useful she could be and he was also well aware of her professional activity at local, regional, and national associations.

The dean had high expectations and no one expected what would happen next. All of the feedback was negative. Librarians and library assistants knew this was their opportunity to prevent an immature, impatient, and selfish woman from becoming the new associate dean. The librarians and staff were grateful for the chance to share what had been happening in the library for the past 10 years. Some of the participants feedback:

- The DC even before being made DC was already a known to be a favorite of the previous library dean. She was an untouchable
- As soon she became a DC she overstepped her power as the DC. She was demanding without ever giving clear directions
- At department meetings, anyone who speaks up needs to be on her side or else. She's always right, interrupts constantly, and is very unprofessional. Many in the library are afraid of her and resent how poorly she treats them. Everyone knows she talks negatively about everyone in the library including the previous dean

- Everyone is worthless according to her. Projects and ideas that represent her department all have to go through her. She is very insecure and enjoys mistreating others in order to feel better about herself
- The DC rides on the backs of new hardworking librarians and steals their work and presents it as her own. She's super passive-aggressive

The dean was shocked to find out what had been going for the past decade. He had only been there a little under 2 years at this point. Everyone liked him, thus his employees had no reason to make him aware of the toxic stress untenured librarians in the instruction department had to endure.

> Between the old Dean and the DC, I think they diluted my self-confidence. When I started at this institution I had much more confidence. I really felt positive about the future and things could only get better from here, but the expectations the DC had for us were so high and without much direction or support…Everyone knew the DC had done way less to earn her tenure.

The dean was not able to promote the DC to associate dean due to the information revealed during the feedback session. Also, because the DC was confident she would get the associate dean position she did not bother to reapply to become the chair of the department for another three-year term. Left with nothing the DC became a regular librarian again after 6 years of being the DC. She no longer had any position of power in the library and, worst of all, no one to advocate for her.

Finally, it was known that she does not talk to any peers, and librarians do not want to work with her on any committees because she is known to be vindictive and they do not want her to accumulate any influence again. She continues to be extremely bitter and feels betrayed. She does not understand why her peers would turn their back on her. She completely dismisses the accusations against her and justifies her horrible behavior by expressing that her mentoring style maybe singular but it makes for better librarians in the end. She was no longer considered a star of the academic library world and could no longer exert influence yet even powerless the old DC makes the librarians around her uncomfortable. The instruction department librarians are excited because they know she is interviewing at other universities and know she will be leaving soon.

It should be noted that this happened in a very large library and because of its multi-department setup the instruction department librarians, even though they were under duress working for a toxic leader, were able to continue serving as best they could all of their users. They were also able to seek advice from their union representatives and their colleagues in other library departments. There was turnover, librarians left, but new librarians were always hired. This is one luxury smaller academic libraries do not have and why it takes longer to notice what is happening in a larger academic library than it is in small-to-medium one as was stated by a librarian who left for a smaller institution believing toxic leadership could not happen in smaller or religiously affiliated institutions. Exit interviews were skipped by many of those who left the institution because they did not want to relive their negative experience. Had these librarians filled out exit interviews perhaps the old library dean would have had to talk to the DC about her toxic leadership style, but knowing that the library dean chose the DC precisely because of her special leadership potential, librarians still at the institution do not believe anything good would have happened in their department.

DISCUSSION QUESTIONS

1. What else could the librarians do to improve their circumstances?
2. Should the department toxic leader be integrated into the librarian's work circle or moved to a special assignment to enable change in the library?
3. What characteristics make the DC a toxic leader?

REFERENCE

Polkinghorne, D. E. (1995). Narrative configuration in qualitative analysis. *Qualitative Studies in Education*, 8(1), 5—23.

CONCLUSION

Toxic leadership does in fact exist in academic libraries, but fortunately not in most (although some academic librarians would declare that it has manifested in too many). What to do with this? The issue of toxic leadership in academic libraries, while it is a reality, has yet to take over the majority of academic libraries; hence the sooner academic libraries accept that ignoring this problem aids in the shuffling of these toxic library leaders, the sooner the real work of stopping it can start. Academic librarians at all types of institutions need to accept that the problem exists. It is not yet fully known how big the problem actually is. The study upon which this book is based on revealed that approximately two-thirds (65.4%) of the librarians who participated had either witnessed or experienced toxic leadership in their careers as academic librarians. The effects of negative, bad, ineffective, and even (in some circumstances) incompetent leadership provide an opportunity for toxic leadership to propagate and have deleterious consequences in the academic library. Problems such as toxic leadership are only solved based on the quality of the leadership trying to ameliorate it. Toxic leadership has long-lasting effects because by the time it is acknowledged it has usually permeated every level of the library. Thus far the effects have been more noticeable in smaller libraries and if it has been permitted to occur for more than 5 years.

Many academic librarians believe that it is time to deal with the repercussions of the poor preparation library schools undertake to teach about leadership and management. The lack of training and mentoring opportunities for mid-career and older librarians is also a continual problem. These more experienced librarians should be the focus of attention because these are the librarians who will potentially become the next library directors, meaning the new leaders and advocates academic libraries desperately need. Mentoring continues to be heavily focused on new librarians, which, although helpful, does a disservice to more experienced librarians, when they are all of a sudden put in positions of power simply because they are good at their jobs and not because they can actually lead or manage. Library schools and professional library associations can and should do more.

Academic librarians are an intelligent and hardworking group of people. They can do more, but they deserve better leadership overall.

Librarians can only do so much on their own if they are not natural leaders, which is why mentoring competent librarians with leadership potential, at all levels, is important. For a true positive impact in the academic library, library leaders who want to make a positive change and who want to advocate for libraries are seriously needed. Toxic leadership, as already mentioned, does not happen in a vacuum. Permissive conditions have to already exist at institutions of higher education in order to enable toxic leaders to flourish, and the same is true for positive change. All academic librarians deserve to work in a healthy library work environment where they can perform their duties and engage in their passions, their calling, without having to worry about being punished for doing their jobs.

Librarians would not have "hung in there" if they did not believe their libraries could improve. This is why library leaders and institutions of higher education need to demonstrate they care by providing oversight, as well as providing adequate funding and strong positive leadership to guarantee that if toxic leadership were to manifest itself again it would be excised immediately. This is an easier task if basic policies and protocols that protect academic librarians are already in place. Toxic leadership in academic libraries does not need to be tolerated more than it already has been, and the work to eradicate it will be easier once librarians are taken seriously and start to be included in the process.

APPENDIX A

Survey Results

A.1 DEMOGRAPHICS

Number of participants: 530 librarians, 492 from the United States. Data provided is about the 492 United States respondents:

Gender: As reflected in the literature, the staffing make-up of the field of Libraries and Information Studies is over 80% female and so were the respondents to this study. Out of 492 respondents, only four did not answer the gender question.

Gender distribution

Gender	Frequency	Percent
Females	427	81.5
Males	87	17.7
Total	488	99.2
Missing	4	0.8
Total	492	100

Race/ethnicity distribution of participants

Race/ethnicity	Frequency	Percent
White/Caucasian	407	82.8
African American	11	2.2
Hispanic	21	4.3
Asian	8	1.6
Native American	4	0.8
Other, please specify	13	2.6
Prefer not to answer	27	5.5
Total	491	99.8
Missing	1	0.2
Total	492	100

A.1.1 Country of Residency

This study focused on academic librarians residing in the United States, 492 librarians (93%) declared the United States as their country of residence. Owing to the posting of the survey link on listservs, there were respondents from other countries, such as: Afghanistan 1 (0.2%), Algeria 1 (0.2%), Australia 2 (0.4%), Canada 13 (02.64%), Hong Kong 1 (0.2%), Jamaica 1 (0.2%), Mexico 18 (03.65%).

Age distribution of participants

Age (years)	Frequency	Percent
18–24	1	0.2
25–30	42	8.5
31–35	48	9.8
36–40	50	10.2
41–45	63	12.8
46–50	61	12.4
51–55	57	11.6
56–60	77	15.7
61–65	53	10.8
66–70	24	4.9
71–75	3	0.6
76 +	1	0.2
Total	480	97.6
Missing	12	2.4
Total	492	100

Public or private institution

Type of institution	Frequency	Percent
Public institutions	314	63.8
Private institutions	175	35.6
Total	489	99.4
Missing	3	00.6
Total	492	100

Academic library type (491 responses out of 492, with only one missing for a total of 99.8%)

Type of library	Frequency	Percent
University libraries	308	62.6
Academic libraries	103	20.9
Law libraries	35	7.1
Research libraries	19	3.9
Community College libraries	10	2.0
Seminary/Theological libraries	4	0.8
Liberal Arts College/4-year college libraries	3	0.6
Medical libraries	2	0.4
Profit College libraries	2	0.4
Special Collections library	1	0.2
Archives	1	0.2
Special library	1	0.2
Total	491	99.8
Missing	1	0.2
Total	492	100

A.2 LEADERSHIP AND TOXIC LEADERSHIP ITEMS

Experienced a toxic leader or supervisor by gender

Gender	Yes	No	Total respondents	Total %
Female	258 (52.9%)	143 (29.3%)	401	82.2%
Male	61 (12.5%)	26 (5.3%)	87	17.8%
Total	319 (65.4%)	169 (34.6%)	488	100%

Schmidt's (2014) Toxic Leadership Scale—Adapted. This toxic leadership scale is comprised of five subscales: Unpredictability, Narcissism, Authoritarian Leadership, Abusive Supervision, Self-promotion. The highest-ranking scales were Unpredictability, Narcissism, and Authoritarian Leadership, in that order. Abusive Supervision and Self-promotion came in fourth and fifth places.

Out of 15 toxic leadership behaviors the most common behaviors (5 highest, 1 lowest) were:

1. Leader varied his/her degree of approachability—Unpredictability (4)
2. Leader allowed his/her current mood to define the climate of the workplace—Unpredictability (4)
3. Leader thought he/she was more capable than others—Narcissism (4)

4. Leader controlled how subordinates completed their tasks—Authoritarian Leadership (4)
5. Leader accepted credit for successes that did not belong to —him/her—Self-promotion (3.5)
6. Leader held subordinates responsible for things outside their job descriptions—Abusive Supervision (3.5)
7. Leader had a sense of personal entitlement—Narcissism (3.5)
8. Leader determined all decisions in the unit whether they were important or not—Authoritarian Leadership (3.5)

Leadership short answer responses:

1. If you can, briefly describe the characteristics of the best leader or leaders you have worked with in an academic library.
2. How, if at all, did the best leader(s) influence the work environment in the library?
3. What is (are) the best leader's(s') gender(s): Male/female (drop down)
4. If you can, briefly describe the characteristics of a problematic leader or leaders you have worked with in an academic library.
5. How, if at all, did the problematic leader(s) influence the work environment in the library? In your opinion, how did the leader's(s') style (s) impact the library environment?
6. What was the problematic leader's(s') gender(s)? Male/female [drop down]
7. Sometimes it is not (or not just) the leader who is problematic in terms of a library's operation. Have you ever had a problematic co-worker when working in an academic library? Yes/No
8. If so, please describe what the co-worker did as well as the impact of his/her actions.

All of the leaders manifested more than one of these behaviors at once and continually, which is what made them toxic leaders. Two-thirds of the survey participants have either experienced or witnessed toxic leadership in their academic libraries.

APPENDIX B

Semi-Structured Interview Guide

Questions:
1. How long have you been at the library and what do you do?
2. Describe the atmosphere at the library during the toxic leadership period.
3. How were you treated at the library?
4. How did you perceive others were treated at the library?
5. How did the environment affect your work?
6. Tell me of an incident in which a crisis was handled well.
7. Tell me of an incident in which a concerning situation was not handled appropriately.
8. Were you given guidance on how to deal with what was going on? If so, of what type?
9. What were the consequences of this environment, in your opinion?
10. In retrospect what would you do differently, if anything?
11. Is there anything else that you would like to add?

INDEX

Printed in the United States
By Bookmasters